Daddies Shouldn't Breakdance

Keep
Breakdancing!
-
signature

Daddies Shouldn't Breakdance

Jimmy Mak

With a foreword by Garrett Morris

Jimmy Mak is the head writer for Shadowbox Live, the largest resident theater company in America, located in Columbus, Ohio. In addition to writing hundreds of comedy sketches seen by hundreds of thousands of patrons, he's also penned a number of original musicals that have been performed for audiences as large as eight thousand people. His plays have been produced in New York, LA, and Hong Kong. On the personal side, Jimmy loves comedy, comic books, records, and the word "pithy." He admits he's not afraid to cry at movies, TV shows, or infomercials. He lives in Gahanna, Ohio, with his wife and two daughters.

Buzz Crisafulli is a recovering business professional who is in the process of turning his life over to the arts, which is probably what he should have done all along. Buzz is a bassist at Shadowbox Live, but he is also building a strong reputation for his photography. His work emphasizes the "extraordinary ordinary," which means finding something special in everyday places and things that people usually take for granted. When he's not playing shows or taking pictures, Buzz is usually watching classic movies or trying to find time to bust loose for that epic continental road trip. He lives in Columbus, Ohio, with his wife and two daughters.

All stories and poems written by Jimmy Mak
Original photography by Buzz Crisafulli
Cover design by Lindsey Bowes
Project management by Donathin Frye

ISBN-13: 9781534918337
ISBN-10: 1534918337
Library of Congress Control Number: 2016910686
CreateSpace Independent Publishing Platform
North Charleston, South Carolina

For Lydia, Riley, and Rosalyn.
Someday I hope to be as funny as you.

Fatherhood is great because you can ruin someone from scratch.
—JON STEWART

I don't dance for anybody but myself.
—OZONE
(FROM THE MOVIE *BREAKIN'*)

CONTENTS

FOREWORD

As head writer for Shadowbox Live, America's largest and greatest resident theater group, Jimmy Mak has been making people laugh for more than twenty years.

As someone who has performed in a number of his sketches over those years, I can tell you that his comedy is as good as, *and may be better than*, anything we were doing on *Saturday Night Live* during the first five years.

Now I realize that this is a bold statement; we did some really funny shit! But believe me, I'm telling you something I know about. When we began working together in 2006, at first I wondered why Shadowbox Live's executive producer, Stev Guyer, had the paperboy talking to me about the sketches I would be performing. Then a few moments later, I met Jimmy Mak's beautiful and supertalented wife, Lydia, and I thought to myself, *Wow…this white boy has game!*

A short while later, I was listening to him go on and on about how he would run home from middle school to catch reruns of original *SNL* episodes. Then he asked me to sign a copy of my musical record album, *Black Creole Chronicles*, and my thoughts were more along the lines of *Nope. No way this nerd has any game.*

So Jimmy gave me the scripts, and soon we were rehearsing and then performing his sketches. By the conclusion of the very successful and hilarious show, I was convinced.

Not only does the boy have game—*Jimmy Mak is my motherfucker!*

Now I can tell you something else I know about. If you read this book, *Daddies Shouldn't Breakdance*, and hopefully head to Columbus, Ohio, to catch a comedy show at Shadowbox Live, Jimmy Mak will absolutely become your motherfucker too.

But seriously, Lydia, you should call me.

Enjoy!

Garrett Morris

Garrett Morris is a comedian and actor. He was part of the original cast of the sketch comedy pro-gram Saturday Night Live, *appearing from 1975 to 1980.*

PREFACE

So here we are. Not too long ago, I was going through my "memory bin"—a bin holding papers, photographs, love letters, news articles, and other stuff that is important to me. I found a plethora of my writings: short stories, poems, and letters from my college days. You'll be happy to know that none of those are in here. But it made me realize something—before I was a "writer," I was a writer.

In the twenty years I've worked at Shadowbox Live, most of my time has been spent writing comedy sketches, plays, and musicals for this remarkable organization. However, sometimes when I had a free moment (which wasn't often), I would write down some story from my past, something silly for my wife, a random thought I had, or a poem for my daughters. These are the writings I have collected in this book.

Many stories happened pretty much as I describe them. I've embellished some for comedic effect. As my good friend David Whitehouse likes to say, "Never let the truth get in the way of a good story."

Hopefully, these stories are good. Hopefully, they make you laugh. Some may make you cry—but even if that's the case, I hope you cry with a smile on your face (the best way to cry). I can't thank you enough for helping me realize this dream. I don't take you for granted.

Sincerely,
Jimmy Mak

I. SOMEWHAT SILLY

DADDIES SHOULDN'T BREAKDANCE

Whether it's Boogaloo Shrimp's surprisingly homoerotic performance as the jilted best friend, the classic Romeo-and-Juliet-in-the-hood subplot, or the stupid-fresh dance moves, it would be hard to deny that the film *Breakin'* is not very good.

But in 1984, at the ripe age of thirteen, I seriously considered it to be the greatest movie of all time. Had I known who Orson Welles was (besides being the giant mass of a person at the end of *The Muppet Movie*), I would have pictured him sitting through the pop locks and body waves in complete and envious awe, his mouth agape. True, it was probably agape because of the popcorn, nachos, and hot dogs he was shoveling into it, but agape nonetheless. I imagine seeing the final images of the movie reflected in Orson's eyes—a neon-graffiti spectacle as Turbo, Ozone, and Special K break in unison. The image goes to black except for the simple words "Coming Soon—*Breakin' 2: Electric Boogaloo*," which causes Orson to spit out his food and utter the ultimate praise: "Word."

When I was growing up, there were two things that saved me from being pummeled by the older kids.

First off, I could usually make them laugh. I did impressions of teachers and other kids at school, and it never failed to get a great reaction from the older students. One time I was on a roll and decided to slip into an impersonation of Groucho Marx, whom my dad believed to be the funniest man in the world.

"I can see you now, bending over a hot stove," I said, doubling over into Groucho's posture, holding a fake cigar and wiggling my eyebrows up and down. "But I can't see the stove."

I stood in silence as the older kids' eyes went from blankness, to confusion, to something like anger. Acting on instinct, I turned into the biology teacher Mr. Columbo and said, "Today I'll be giving a lecture on how to dissect a fart." Big laugh (and an important lesson on the seemingly timeless and universal appreciation of flatulence humor).

The second reason I didn't get beaten up was that I could breakdance. I have no idea how my superskinny, white, suburban body was able to learn and fine-tune the breakdance vocabulary, but there I was—worming and spidering and crabwalking and twisting into a plethora of contortions, all named after small, disgusting creatures. This was a big hit with the tall, muscular African-American kids at the middle school, who invited me to join in their break circle.

A break circle was basically a group of young men who would do a kind of a skip-step around a piece of cardboard until someone (no doubt inspired by the intricate sounds of

"Roxanne, Roxanne" by UTFO—only the greatest rap song ever made) would jump in the middle and proceed to get down with his bad self. The other guys in my break circle had names like Smoov D, Papa Smurf, and Jingle Bear (who wisely renamed himself MC Kill a year later). Refusing to breakdance with "Jimmy," they soon handed me the moniker of Phantom J, which was and will always be the coolest nickname I've ever had.

Whereas being funny had always made me kind of goofy, being able to breakdance made me kind of cool. I would go to the skating rink on Saturday afternoons, and for fifteen minutes, they

would clear the floor, play some rap, and let the kids breakdance. It was there I found my signature finish: I would walk around on my hands, using my elbows to hold myself up, legs bent backward in the air to balance me—this move was called the crabwalk and was a feat unto itself. Then I would slide onto my back, roll back onto my shoulders, and push off the ground, thus propelling me onto my feet. This move was called a kip and could be seen in any kung-fu movie. I called it the crabwalk-kip combo. And I'll be honest: it got me more than one girlfriend (Tricia, Cassie, and, um…hey, two's more than one).

When the film *Breakin'* came to the theater just blocks from my house, my friend Jamie and I saw it approximately 314 times. We had it memorized. We quoted it like it was a Monty Python movie. We studied the moves. Like my imaginary Orson, when the end of the movie promoted *Breakin' 2*, we enthusiastically worded it up.

Now I don't remember when it happened, but breakdancing did go out of style. However, I never forgot my moves. The only difference was that now instead of making me cool, they made me even goofier. Breakdancing had become funny. Needless to say, my groupies dissipated, and I went back to being that somewhat weird but safe guy girls would talk to about their boyfriends and remind constantly he was "like a brother" to them.

Twenty years later: I was working as a writer/performer for Shadowbox, a theater that specializes in sketch comedy and rock n' roll shows. We were putting together a Christmas production, and we decided that the band would do a version of Run DMC's "Christmas in Hollis." (If you've never heard this song, please don't feel the need to purchase it. I have too many things to feel guilty about and would rather not add that to the list.) The choreographer decided to add a dance to go with the rap, and somehow she found out that I could breakdance. She asked to see my moves, and I showed her. She was impressed—so much so that she gave me a solo: four eight-counts to do whatever breakdance moves I wanted.

I guess I should also mention that at the time, I had just become a father, and the most exercise I did was to try to push my wife out of bed when the baby was crying. In other words, my body wasn't exactly the same body that folded and twisted and leapt and spun all those years ago.

We started rehearsing, and when it got to my solo, I ran to the front of the group. I popped. I locked. I waved. I wormed. I spun. I crabwalked. I kipped. I fell. I hurt. I cried.

I was lying crumpled up on the carpeted stage, wondering how my body was ever going to forgive me, when one of the younger guys in the dance walked over and looked down at me. I was waiting for him to ask if I was OK, but all he said was, "Dude, daddies shouldn't breakdance."

That was a hard moment for me. I had always been a firm believer in the *Breakin' 2: Electric Boogaloo* tagline, which was "If you can't beat the system…break it!" However, I felt a little different about it when the system happened to be my spine.

CHAPTER 2

THE BUBBA JIM CHRONICLES

Part 1—Howdy, Neighbor!

Be careful what you wish for.
I'm not sure who originally came up with this saying. Some say it goes all the way back to Noah, who, as a child, was heard to utter, "I sure do like water. I wish there was more of it." Regardless, the saying is true.

Believe me.

No, seriously.

It all started when my wife and I bought a house. It was a house in what they call a "transitional neighborhood." Transitioning toward something or away from something, I wasn't really sure. Half of the houses on the street were cute little homes, and half were ready to fall down at any second. Our house was a cute little home, but it was bookended by the two worst-looking houses on the street.

The house to our left looked as if it was barely held together. Every once in a while, we'd see a very old man shuffle out and get the mail.

"I sure wish they'd fix up that house," I told my wife.

Two months later, there was a crew of guys at the house next door, fixing it up. There was also a "For Rent" sign in the front yard.

"What do you think happened to the old man?" my wife asked.

"I think some people came and took him to a farm where he can run free all day and finally be happy," I replied. My wife is a very sensitive woman.

They painted the house next door and put new siding on. It started to look really good.

A couple mornings later, my wife and I were sleeping but were jarred awake when we heard a sound louder than anything I'd ever heard before. The sound was this: "Fuuuuuuuuuucccccccccccccccckkkkkkkkkkk!"

Then there was a crash.

I peeked out my window to see the heavyset bald man who had been working on the roof next door stumble out of the neighbor's house and into the yard.

He pulled out his phone or walkie-talkie and hit the button.

Beep, beep. "Darlene! Is Bob there?"

Muffled response.

Beep, beep. "You need to tell him that this whole fuckin' roof is rotted out."

Muffled response.

Beep, beep. "Yes, I'm fuckin' sure!"

Muffled response.

Beep, beep. "'Cause I just fuckin' fell through it!"

Later that day, I was out in the backyard, and the guy was back on the roof next door. He saw me and shouted down, "I'm fixing up this house!"

"I see that," I replied.

"I fell through this fuckin' roof three times," he said excitedly, a big smile on his face showing that his mouth contained no top teeth.

"Well, you need to be careful," I said.

"Fuck, yeah!"

I noticed that he had been throwing pieces of the bad roof along the side of my house, on my property. He saw what I was looking at.

"Hey, buddy, I'll try and get those later. Prolly not today." Then his phone beeped, and he began another shouting conversation into his walkie. I believe he even said a few words other than "fuck."

The next day, I cleaned the side of my house of the debris. The roof-faller had been dubbed "Bubba Jim" by my wife. This is not intended to offend anyone out there named Bubba Jim. It just seemed to fit. Unlike most of his clothes.

After a week of listening to Bubba Jim having nonstop explosive arguments with his radio-phone, I told my wife, "God, I can't wait until that house is finished."

A couple days later, it was. Bubba Jim was gone. The little house that was ready to collapse actually looked nice. We hoped for decent neighbors.

I came home from work not too long after that, and as I got out of my car, I heard a familiar sound.

Beep, beep. "Well, just tell him to hold his fuckin' horses, and I'll be there when I'm good and goddamn ready!"

I looked up to see Bubba Jim standing in the front yard of the neighbor's house, holding the "For Rent" sign. He was wearing paint-splattered sweat pants, ripped socks, and no shirt. He saw me and smiled his huge, toothless grin.

"Howdy, neighbor!" he shouted.

Part 2—God Made Dirt; Dirt Don't Hurt

It wasn't long before I realized that Bubba Jim's falling through the roof three times was just a normal day at the office for him.

My first real conversation with him was when we both got home from work at the same time. I got out of my car, and he got out of his truck, and we both headed toward our houses. I knew he was staring at me, so I finally looked over.

"How's it going?" I asked.

"Fell out of a tree," he replied.

"I'm sorry?"

"Fell out a goddamn tree. I was up like two hundred feet trimming these trees, and I fell."

"Jesus, are you OK?" I asked.

"Had to go to the hospital. Busted up my ribs. They tried to tell me not to go to work, but I said, 'Fuck that.' You know what I mean?"

I assured him that I did.

"Yeah, man," he continued. "One minute I'm way up there…" He pointed upward so I was clear on the direction he was referring to. "And the next—*pow*—I'm on the dirt."

"Well, I'm glad you're all right," I said, not sure if I meant it.

"Well, hell," he said. "God made dirt, and dirt don't hurt, right?"

I was going to tell him I didn't think his scenario necessarily fit the children's rhyme, but I thought better of it. He was looking up at the two tall trees I had in my front yard.

"I can trim those for you," he offered. I declined.

Soon after that, his truck broke down. However, that didn't stop him from trying to start it using a clever and original tactic—he just kept turning the key and gunning the gas in the hopes the engine would turn over. He did this for three days.

It seemed every ten minutes we'd hear *reahhhhh, reahhhhh, reahhhh,* followed by "Fuck!"

"God, I wish he'd get that truck fixed," I told my wife. (Why can't I learn not to wish for stuff?)

The next day, the truck was in several pieces in his backyard. As he worked to get it fixed, he coined a new word—*shfuck.* He said this quite a bit. I imagine that it started with him starting to say "shit" and then realizing halfway through that the situation deserved "fuck." By the way, "shfuck" fits so many more circumstances than I thought; it's now one of those words my iPhone recognizes.

He got the truck fixed. It seemed to do things a truck was supposed to—move forward, backward, and stop. The problem was that now the truck made an incredibly loud racket. The only way I can describe it is to say that it sounded like a chainsaw cutting into another running chainsaw.

The next day, I saw him in his front yard as I was getting into my car.

"I see you got your truck fixed," I said.

"Yeah, but you know what?"

I didn't, so I said, "What?"

"I was under the goddamn thing, and it slid off the fucking jack and ran over my wrist. And now"—he used his other hand to move his wrist back and forth—"I got no feeling in my wrist. Look, I can't feel this. Is that bad?"

"I don't think it's good," I replied. "You might want to get that looked at."

"Fuck that," he said.

"Yeah, I know what you mean."

I got in my car and drove off, watching him in my rearview mirror as he just kept looking at his wrist like a confused dog.

The next day, his kids showed up.

———◆———

Part 3—That Truck Ain't No Monkey Bars

As I pulled up to my house, I saw the familiar sight of Bubba Jim's pickup. Only something about it was different. The back windshield had been smashed out, but that wasn't it. The side mirror had been knocked loose and was dangling by a chord next to the car door, but that wasn't it. There were four little girls jumping in the bed of the truck as if it were a trampoline. That was it.

They were all screaming at the top of their lungs and gave the neighborhood (which up to this point had been pretty quiet) a new air, kind of like a prison riot had just broken out.

I pulled up in front of the playground-truck and got out of my car. The girls stopped what they were doing and looked at me.

"Hi," I said.

They each gave me a look as if I were Turbo, who had foolishly moonwalked through Electro Shock's section of the 'hood. (I'm sure you all get that *Breakin'* reference, right?) Then they went back to shouting and jumping. Before I reached my door, Bubba Jim oozed out of his front door wearing his classic bright-pink sweatpants complemented nicely by nothing else.

"Hey, neighbor!" he shouted as if I were four houses away. "I got my girls here now."

"Really?" I asked, trying to joke with him. "Where are they?"

His eyebrows went down in the middle. "Right there," he said, pointing at his truck and wondering why he had to move next door to a complete idiot.

"Hey, girls," he shouted as one of the girls was climbing onto the roof of the cab. "That truck ain't no monkey bars. Get out of there; one of you could get hurt."

I started thinking that maybe I had been too hard on Bubba Jim. I mean, after all, he had four girls to take care of and seemed concerned with their safety. Sure, he was loud. He cussed a lot. He was accident-prone. But that didn't mean he was a bad person.

One of the little girls jumped from the roof of the cab into the bed of the truck. Bubba Jim turned red before he shouted, "I said get away from that fucking truck before I beat your fucking asses, goddammit!"

My eyes widened, and Bubba Jim gave me that "kids…what are you gonna do?" look. The girls jumped out of the truck and headed for their new home. One of the girls (who seemed about eight years old) replied, "Well, there ain't nothing to fucking do in this shit hole!" The four disappeared into the tiny house, and the door slammed.

"Hey," said Bubba Jim, suddenly smiling in the friendliest way. "Maybe my girls and your girl can get together later and play."

Part 4—You're Never Too Old, Right?

It was a few days before Halloween and just starting to get cool. My dad was supposed to come visit and take my family to dinner, but his car broke down two blocks from his house, and he had to cancel. So I decided to cook out. I was at the grill while my daughter Riley was coloring on the patio with sidewalk chalk. Suddenly we heard the window slide open at Bubba Jim's house. Riley and I looked up to see a girl maybe six years old staring at us.

"It's no fun to be locked up in your room," she said.

I told her that I imagined that to be true.

"Whatcha doin'?" she asked me.

"Cooking out," I said.

"My pap-pap was supposed to come see me, but his car broke down," explained Riley.

"Well, my grandma's dead," replied the girl.

"She's got you beat," I told Riley.

"That smells good," said the girl. "What is that, meatballs?"

"Chicken," I replied.

"You think you're gonna have a lot of leftovers?" she asked.

The next day was Beggar's Night. I had to work until six, so my wife took Riley to trick-or-treat in her friend's neighborhood. I picked up some candy on my way home to hand out to the little ghouls and goblins that would soon be roaming the streets.

In no time, I heard a large crowd heading up my walkway. I picked up my bowl of M&Ms and SweeTARTS and looked out my front door. Bubba Jim and his four girls were approaching (none of them wearing costumes) and screaming over one another. The only thing I could make out was Bubba Jim saying, "Well, it ain't no fucking contest!"

He looked up and saw me.

"Trick-or-treat, neighbor!" he screamed, and they all held out pillowcases.

I noticed Bubba Jim was also holding one out.

"You're never too old, right?" he asked.

The sad part was I actually believed that to be true until that very moment. I gave them each some candy.

"Oh, hey," said Bubba Jim, "I got two nieces that are real sick and stuff, and they couldn't come with us tonight. Can you go on and give me a couple more extras so I can take 'em back to 'em?"

Later that night, I was sitting on my front porch drinking a beer when I heard the familiar sound of a jackhammer trying to go through sheet metal. Bubba Jim's truck appeared from the darkness and barreled up over the curb and onto the sidewalk. Bubba Jim dropped out and stormed to his door, screaming into his phone, "No, he's in fucking jail again! I don't fucking know; it wasn't even real anyway."

His door slammed. I worked very hard trying not to figure out what he was talking about. I sighed and wondered if Bubba Jim planned on living there for the long term. I decided to look at the positives. Um…hmmmm. Oh, well, his house looked pretty good. I mean it used to look like a shack held together with packaging tape, but now it actually looked like a cute little house. So there was that.

Suddenly his door opened again, and he walked out onto his porch with a big-barrel plastic garbage can and threw its contents onto his front yard. In the blink of an eye, his yard was decorated with McDonald's bags and cans of Milwaukee's Best Light. The new look must not have pleased him as he'd hoped, because then he angrily tossed the now-empty garbage can down before disappearing back into his house.

It occurred to me then how much more money McDonald's would make if they actually sold Milwaukee's Best Light.

———✦———

Part 5—I Love My Grilz

One morning, I woke up to a very strange sound. There was a surreal quality to it, like it wasn't meant to exist, and just hearing it made me question what was real and what wasn't. The sound was Bubba Jim and his children laughing. Hearing this large ball of toothless anger suddenly express joviality was as disturbing as hearing Pope Francis reading the audio book version of *Fifty Shades of Grey*. I peeked out my window to see what was going on. I half expected Bubba Jim to be watching for me, only to yell, "Ha-ha, fooled you!" and then go right back to calling his daughter a bitch-bag.

But there they were. He had his arm around one of his daughters. He was smiling. He had a shirt on!

What the shfuck is going on? I thought.

That's when I noticed he was talking to a professional-looking woman with a clipboard standing in his yard.

"Well, you seem to be doing really well," she said, heading to her car.

Who was she? Children's Services? Church volunteer? An alien who came down here looking for intelligent life and was heading home disappointed? Whoever she was, I wanted to run out, tackle her, and scream, "He's not doing well! It's an act! Make it go away, Clipboard Lady, make it go away!" But then—just like Bubba Jim's teeth, hair, and soul—she was gone.

Later that day, I was in my front yard raking some leaves when Bubba Jim's truc (the *k* is missing because so was the vehicle's bumper, side mirrors, and back windshield) pulled up. He had painted in large black letters the following message on the truc's side: I Love My Grilz.

At first I thought about my grill and how I do love it—just not enough to write on my car about it. Then I realized he meant his "girls." Wow, so maybe he was scared of Clipboard Lady and was really going to try to be on his best behavior.

"Hey, chief," he said when he saw me. "D'you see the cops here last night?"

"No," I said. "Were they here?"

"Don't think so," he said as if my question didn't really make sense. "Yeah, those people down the street broke into my garage and cleaned it out. And I got a ton of shit in there.

Ton of shit that's worth a lot of fuckin' money. So I went downtown to fill out a report and call the cops."

I was going to point out that normally people didn't have to travel downtown to call the police but thought better of it.

"But when I got home," he continued, "they had put all my stuff back."

"So they broke into your garage, took everything, but then put it all back when you weren't home?" I asked.

"Yep. Fucking Junebug," he replied. I figured the less I knew about Junebug, the better. "And I'm trying to be good here," he continued, "'cause the last place I lived? Well, shit, you don't want to know."

For once, Bubba Jim was right.

I hoped that he was serious about trying to be good. It had been pretty quiet over there the last few days, but I wasn't holding my breath. Well, technically, I *was* holding my breath because he smelled like a mixture of fish and urinal cakes.

At two in the morning, we heard several loud banging noises and screaming. A strange man (Junebug?) was at Bubba Jim's door pounding as hard as he could.

"Get out here right now, you bald, toothless motherfucker!" he screamed.

My wife and I moved our kids to the kitchen and called the cops. We heard glass breaking and more pounding.

"Settle the fuck down!" screamed Bubba Jim.

"Kill that fucker!" screamed his grilz.

—•—

Part 6—You Got Mudded

"You work on computers or somethin'?"

Bubba Jim was sitting on a folding chair in the middle of his front yard. I was carrying my laptop into the house.

"Uh, no," I replied. "Why, do you have a computer that needs fixing?"

"Fuck, no," he answered concisely and a little too passionately. "I just see you with that computer all the time."

"Oh, well, I'm a writer."

Suddenly he contorted his hands into big broken spiders and mockingly yelled out, "Oooh, look at me. I got carpal tunnel, I got carpal tunnel!"

I wasn't sure how to respond, so I just stared at him. He must have thought I didn't understand, because he quickly replied, "It's a real thing. First time I heard someone say it, I thought they meant a tunnel in the carpool lane, but it's really like finger cramps or something."

I went inside my house, where it was a little more unstupid.

At six in the morning, an explosion of anger erupted from next door. The curse words hit my bedroom window like hail. Bubba Jim seemed to be having trouble getting his grilz ready for school at a speed that pleased him.

"Get! The fuck! Ready! You're! Fucking! Late! Damn! Fuck! Now!"

I slowly started to get out of bed to ask him to kindly turn it down a notch or seven, but by the time I got to the front door, his truc came to coughing life and sped down the street.

This continued for about a week. One morning, I was a little more on top of my game and jumped out of bed and ran to the front porch. Bubba Jim was standing in the street, screaming at his grilz, who were still in the house.

"Move your goddamn asses! Let's gooooooooooo!"

"Hey!" I screamed. He glanced at me, surprised. "You think you might be able to keep it down in the mornings? You're waking up the entire house here."

"Oh, yeah, neighbor," he said apologetically. "I didn't think you could hear that."

"I think the whole neighborhood could hear that," I replied and went back inside.

The next morning, it was quiet. I felt good. I was afraid that Bubba Jim would be twice as loud out of spite, but it seemed like he was complying without any trouble. I walked outside and noticed our car looking *browner* than normal. Upon closer inspection, I saw that somebody or somebodies had wiped mud all over the windshield and windows. It had obviously been smeared by hand and was caked on thick. I wondered what kind of people would cover themselves in nasty mud just to wipe it on my car.

Bubba Jim and his girls exploded out of the house next door. He saw me inspecting my car, and he came over to join me.

"Oh, shit, neighbor," he said. "You got mudded."

His girls looked like they were holding back laughter. I suddenly pictured Bubba Jim and his girls at two in the morning with a big pot of mud, all of them dipping their hands in it and smearing it on my car, laughing, as if finally finding that something that could bring them together as a family. Maybe it helped them discover some love for each other they never knew they had. I like to believe this is true.

Part 7—Mommy Dirtiest

I was playing with my two daughters in the backyard. Bubba Jim's daughter (the eight-year-old) came running in her backyard, screaming back at her sister, "Shut up, you fucking crack whore!" Then she looked over at us.

"Hey!" she screamed with a big smile. "My dad says I can come over and play there and climb your tree."

"Well, I'm sorry, but you can't," I replied.

"Why not?" she demanded.

I wanted to tell her that it was because I believed Bubba Jim ordered her to climb our tree and fall so he could sue us. Or that I was afraid she was actually going to dirty up the tree. Or, even though calling her sister a "crack whore" may have been an accurate description, I didn't appreciate that language.

Instead, we just went inside. My wife and I then spent the best money we ever spent and got a privacy fence in the backyard.

A month went by (in Bubba Jim time, this means two dogs and three cats later). It was about eleven o'clock at night, and I was taking the trash can from the backyard to put out in the street when I saw a sight that made my heart metaphorically get an erection. It was a large moving truck in front of Bubba Jim's! Was this really happening? I smiled. A small tear lovingly slid down my cheek. Bubba Jim and some other guy (Junebug?) came waddling out of his house—empty handed. My smile started to dissipate as I watched them walk into the truck and carry boxes *inside*.

They weren't moving out. Someone else was moving in with them. It was then I heard the voice, which sounded like a mixture of Loretta Lynn and that guy from the movie *Sling Blade*.

A woman walked out of the house with a big smile on her face. She screamed to one of the grilz standing in the doorway, "Well, hell, you little bitch. I don't give a fuck what you do!"

No, this couldn't be happening.

"Trash, huh?" Bubba Jim suddenly screamed to me.

I was staring at the woman and about to answer "without a doubt" when I realized he was referring to the trash can I was still holding. I nodded, still in disbelief.

"Guess who's outta jail?" he asked with a smile, showing me all his tooth ghosts.

I looked back over at the new lady of the house. She glared at me for one second as if getting a load of the awful neighbor she had heard so much about, stomped out a cigarette, and went back inside.

The next morning, Bubba's house looked like the aftermath of a war zone. Trash, boxes, TVs, giant plastic playground parts, clothes, a microwave, mattresses, and gas cans had been thrown with abandon onto his front yard. I could see through the front window of his house that there were boxes piled everywhere inside. Suddenly, something in the yard made what sounded like a growling or hissing noise or both. It was a cough. Somehow I had failed to notice Mrs. Bubba sitting in a lawn chair in the midst of the debris. She was smoking. I almost pointed out to her that there were gas cans near where she was sitting, but then…then I thought better of it.

She looked over at me. At first I thought she was trying to say hello, but it turned out to be another cough. Then she spit. On her leg.

———◆———

Part 8—The Calm After the Fuck Storm

After a couple of weeks, it became clear that they had no intention of cleaning up their yard, which had taken on the sweet aroma of a dumpster behind a Long John Silvers. On this particular night, it was raining—it was more like a monsoon, actually—and I was running from my car to my house. I noticed Bubba Jim on his front porch admiring all the paper and debris being blown from his swamp-yard out into the neighborhood.

"One helluva fuck storm!" he yelled happily when he saw me.

That was it.

I decided I wasn't going to be pushed around by this hillbilly from hell (hellbilly?) any longer. I took a deep breath, cracked my knuckles, and bravely went inside and called the city to report him.

Shockingly, it turned out there were several other complaints about him, and the next day someone showed up and told him he had two days to clean up the yard.

Two days later, the yard looked the exact same way. I called again. The next day, the man from the city came back and said, "No, seriously, you need to clean this up." I watched with a mix of fascination and disgust as Bubba Jim then went to work moving all the yard trash back into his already-packed house.

A few days later, the rain cleared up.

The wife, kids, and I were in the backyard enjoying the beautiful day and, more importantly, our fence. Suddenly, we heard Bubba in the front yard scream, "Well, how the fuck was I supposed to know this would fuckin' happen two weeks after you fucking moved in here?"

Curious, my family and I walked to the front yard. There was another big moving truck in front of Bubba Jim's house.

"Down, heart erection," I told myself. "We've been through this before."

The grilz walked out of his house, carrying boxes that I could only assume contained a mixture of headless Barbie dolls and discarded banana peels, and put them in the truck.

"Hey, buddy!" Bubba Jim screamed. I looked around for Junebug but then realized he was talking to me. "You better keep your eye out for vandals and shit. Turns out we gotta move."

My wife grabbed my hand and squeezed it. I wasn't sure what the hell vandals had to do with his leaving (except that there would be one less to worry about), but I didn't care. I took the family out to celebrate. We drank. We laughed. We danced. A foul-mouthed, bald, toothless, three-hundred-pound weight had been lifted from us.

And the next day, they were gone. No more grilz, no more truc, no more Mommy Dirtiest. I know this is probably my imagination, but I swear I heard the entire neighborhood simultaneously let out a sigh of relief. The little house was eerily quiet. I stood in the front yard. The sun was shining. I heard a bird chirp. The guy across the street was on his front porch smoking a cigarette. He waved and screamed, "Congratulations!"

I smiled. The fuck storm was over.

———

Epilogue

A month after the Bubbas left, my wife and I decided to move. I'm not sure why we put up with Bubba Jim and the Trashettes for three years before deciding that. Maybe we knew it would be impossible to sell our house with them there, I don't know. Regardless, we ended up moving to a pretty fancy neighborhood. The way I see it, it's our turn to be the Bubba Jims for a change. We sure as shfuck deserve it.

CHAPTER 3

MERRY DISAPPOINTMENT

Like a lot of you, Christmas was a very special time for me when I was a kid. The memories are magical. Who doesn't remember going out on Christmas morning to play in the slush? Or that first moment you take the tree out of the box and spray the pine-scented Lysol around the house? I remember my parents used to drive me downtown near the jail late at night so we could look at all the pretty red and blue flashing lights.

I remember one year, all I wanted was a VCR. This is when they first came out. I said to my parents, "Look, you can forget about all the games and the clothes and the mouthwash you get me every year for some reason. Forget about all that. This year all I want are a VCR and a videotape of the movie *Beat Street* starring Rae Dawn Chong."

They told me no. But come on. How many times did they say no about a gift only to surprise me with it on Christmas morning? OK, never. But I had heard of it happening.

That Christmas morning, I woke up excited but knew that it was early and that my parents would appreciate a little more sleep. So I instantly ran in and woke them up. I walked down the stairs and instead of seeing one big wrapped-up box with my name on it, there were a bunch of little wrapped-up boxes. Well, first I was confused, but then I realized my parents must have just disassembled the VCR and put each part in a little box.

Clever, I thought.

I looked at them and winked. They looked at each other, thoroughly confused.

I opened the first box, and it was underwear. I opened the second box, and it was…a Nancy Drew mystery? I opened the third box, and it was that damn mouthwash. I opened up all my gifts, and there was no VCR.

I could feel myself becoming incredibly upset but calmed down because I thought about Ralphie from *A Christmas Story*. You remember. All he wanted was a BB gun. So he told his parents. They told him no. Then on Christmas morning, he opened up all his gifts, and he thought he didn't get it, but then they surprised him with it.

So I waited a couple of months.

Finally, I realized I wasn't getting a VCR.

I went up to my mom and said, "Mom, where's my VCR? I wanted a VCR! You didn't get me a VCR!"

My mom said to me, "Now, Jimmy, there are poor foreign children who live in caves and eat dirt. And they're thankful for that dirt."

I took this all in—the 1980s guilt-laden admonishment that children from affluent Western countries have to hear whenever they can't get what they want.

And I said, "So? Where's my fucking VCR?"

Unlike Ralphie, I didn't get my present. Like Ralphie, I sucked on soap for an hour.

You'll be happy to know that eventually I did get my VCR. Last year I tried (and failed) to sell it at a yard sale for a quarter. The memory of that Christmas, however, is priceless.

CHAPTER 4

THESE ARE MY THOUGHTS, AND YOU CAN'T HAVE THEM! (SO HERE THEY ARE): PART 1

- Not too long ago, people changed their Facebook profile pictures to cartoon characters as a reminder to be aware of child abuse. Child abuse isn't funny, but cartoons are, so now I'm, like, all confused.
- Many people don't know we had a president for one day named David Rice Atchison. Something else many people don't know is how to drive in the rain.
- The problem, Aretha, is I'd like to give you *a lot* of respect, but you keep insisting I only give you a little bit.

- I don't think the people who say they never take things lying down have actually tried it. I can't imagine a more comfortable way of taking things.
- Lessons I've learned #41: When you're working at a bookstore and someone calls in asking for a book on eunuchs, don't spend a half hour searching for books about castrated men because they mean "Unix," which has its own shelf in the computer section.
- Sometimes I think I'm the only one who's given up on the idea of individualism.
- I'm living the dream. That's right; I'm naked at my middle school right now.
- I am, was, and always will be someone who enjoys writing sentences that use the present, past, and future tenses.
- I wonder if Charles Dickens realized his true legacy would be making sure no kid was named Ebenezer ever again.
- If Westboro Baptist Church doesn't protest my funeral, I know I've done something seriously wrong with my life.
- Call me an optimist, but I think it's nice that so many people who lose cats live next to telephone poles.
- Chances are good when a guy says "*That's* what I'm talking about," he has not been talking about that.
- Everyone seems to focus on the fact that Sir Mix-a-Lot likes big butts. I'm way more impressed that he cannot lie.
- A friend told me he made it to sixth base with his girlfriend. I need to start watching baseball again.
- I was very excited to go see *Princesses on Ice* with my family until I found out that "on ice" in this case didn't mean "dead."
- I hate passive-aggressive people so much I want to hug them.
- I'm pretty sure the phrase I've uttered the most out loud (even more often than "How's it going?" or "See you later!") is "Nice turn signal, asshole."
- Steubenville, Ohio, was once known as Little Chicago. Therefore, I feel it's only fair to start referring to Chicago as "Big Steubenville."
- Isn't *Resident Evil 3D* kind of like just having a big pile of crap thrown in your face?
- I'm not one to complain, but people who start sentences with "I'm not one to complain" usually just end up complaining about something.
- I am not one of those adults who wear a costume on Halloween. I am one of those adults who wear a costume nearly every day of my life.

CHAPTER 5

LIFE WITH RILEY
(WRITTEN ONE WEEK AFTER BECOMING A FATHER)

The Birth

My wife, Lydia, was convinced it was a boy. She said that her "maternal instinct thing" told her so. Or maybe it was how hard the baby kicked her (i.e., very hard). True, she had dreamed it was a girl, but she had also dreamed that Ohio State was going to beat Michigan. They didn't. Therefore, it seemed to follow that her dream about the baby was just as wrong. Me? I was convinced it was a girl. Call it what you will: my paternal instinct thing or the fun of disagreeing with my wife.

The baby was due on December 20, three days before my birthday and five days before Christmas. (Ha-ha, the kid was gonna get screwed at Christmas, just like me!) Anyway, on December 19, my wife and I woke up and were getting ready for work.

"I think my water may have broken," she said to me as I brushed my teeth.

"Weirry?" I replied with a mouthful of toothpaste. "Whrreeiy?"

She told me that she "kind of" leaked but not really (but kind of). She called the doctor's office to let them know, and they told her to come in. We called work, informed them that we might or might not be having a baby, and headed to the hospital.

"This is ridiculous," she said. "I know I'm gonna get there, they're gonna do some tests, get me all comfortable, and then tell me to go home."

"Oh, relax," I said in a soothing voice. "I'm sure they won't get you all comfortable."

We got to the hospital, checked in, and were given a room. It was very much like a hotel in that regard. Lydia was still convinced she was going to be discharged at any second. Some nurses came in and did some tests. We watched television, read magazines, talked about how if she wasn't giving birth, we'd go see the new Lord of the Rings movie, and so on. Our doctor showed up and told us (I'm paraphrasing here) that, yes, Lydia had kind of leaked, and that meant she was kind of in labor. He predicted a baby at around two the next morning (it was currently noon). Then he left.

From about nine thirty that morning to four thirty that afternoon, things were pretty uneventful. She felt normal and acted fine, and I thought that if this is what labor is like, why did they play that movie in baby school? You know, the one where that pregnant woman looks and sounds like she's starring in *The Exorcist Part 7: Demon Semen*? And her husband keeps glancing at the camera like, "Run! Run, you fools!"

Then four thirty hit, and the contractions started. Now, as a man, I'll never know that feeling, but I liken it to sitting at the end of a bowling lane with my legs spread while someone sends the bowling ball careening down the slick surface with extreme speed until it gracefully crushes my nut sack. Over and over again.

Lydia said she would try to go without medication as long as she could stand it, which was approximately up until the first contraction. They gave her this stuff that made her seem very, very drunk. I thought that was sweet because it reminded me of the night the baby was conceived.

Next came the epidural. Either they failed to mention it, or my wife was a little loopy (I wonder which it was) because I guess she's supposed to lie on one side for a while and then the other to make sure she was numb all over. Well, she lay on one side. And stayed on that side. So she could still feel the contractions on one half of her body (for guys, the bowling ball would only hit one testicle). When they figured out what was going on, they gave her a little more juice and had her lie on her other side. Finally, she could feel no pain. (Again, very much like the night the child was conceived.)

At about 9:00 p.m., she was ready to pop. The doctor rushed back in. Thinking he still had a good five hours, he had gone on a date with his wife. (Silly gynecologist.) Suddenly, Lydia was pushing and breathing and pushing and grunting, and Doc asked me if I'd like to catch the baby. Hoping he didn't mean he was going to deliver the child and then toss it to me, I said, "Sure." He showed me how to hold my hands, and the next thing I knew, this…this…person, only smaller, was in my arms.

I remember feeling so many things. Complete joy. Wonder. Awe. Love. But mostly I felt smug. Because I was right. It was a girl.

Newborn

Riley Elizabeth was born at 9:34 p.m. on December 19, 2003. She had a full head of dark-brown hair. She was six pounds, three ounces, and nineteen inches long. She was beautiful.

The room Lydia and I slept in at the hospital had a nice bed for Lydia (naturally), a bassinet for Riley (naturally), and a chair that sort of pulled into a longer chair for me (huh?). Anyway, Lydia and I were both in that state of total exhaustion where we couldn't sleep but were too tired to do anything else. Plus, she couldn't move her legs, so that nixed a lot of activities right there. I stretched out in my chair-plus-more-chair and watched *A Christmas Story* for about the eight hundred and seventeenth time. Then it was time to feed Riley. Then they brought food for Lydia. Then I decided to wait until the next day to eat. Seriously, though, the punishment that fathers get for not actually pushing a small human out of an orifice is called the hospital brush-off.

"Do you got stitches in your privates? No? Then get your own damn food, penis-haver! By the way, how's your bed? Mwuh, ha-ha-ha!"

At about four in the morning, after managing to fall asleep in my Not-Really-All-That-La-Z-Boy, I heard a disturbing crash right next to me. I popped up and saw my wife crumpled on the floor with a nurse over her.

Is this nurse beating up my wife? I thought to myself. *I think I saw a movie about this once. Oh, wait, no, I'm thinking of the movie where the nurses all decide that what their patients really need is…*I'm getting off track.

It turned out that the nurse was helping Lydia out of bed to use the restroom. Half of Lydia's body, it seems, was still completely numb from the epidural, so when she tried to put weight on her foot, she ended up tipping over and crashing to the floor with all the grace of a cartoon anvil.

"Oh, my God," the nurse gasped. "In all my years of nursing, I have never dropped a patient."

I immediately felt a bond with this woman. We were first-time parents, and she was a first-time dropper.

The time you spend in a hospital after the baby is born is completely surreal. I started thinking of it in sci-fi terms: the building itself became something you'd see in a futuristic movie, something called "an identity transfer center." Lydia and I walked into this building as husband and wife with a set way of living. We were about to leave as mother and father, a whole new world waiting.

Taking the baby home has got to be the scariest thing ever. OK, I guess being forced at gunpoint to read Carrot Top's autobiography while the song "You Spin Me Right Round, Baby" plays over and over again is the scariest thing ever. But this is close. You have this tiny person that has been cared for the last couple of days by experts suddenly handed to you with a "good luck." We put all six pounds, three ounces of our daughter in her car seat (which looked like it had room for about twelve more babies her size). We put the car seat in the car. Lydia got in back with her, and I drove slowly and carefully. Lydia cried. I kept checking the rearview mirror, asking every two seconds, "How's she doing?"

Riley Comes Home

The lovely Lydia and I threw ourselves into the art of parenting with verve and zeal. Once we arrived home, we placed the breathing bundle into the bassinet and proceeded to sit on the edge of the bed and stare at her. We did this for weeks.

I had to learn how to change a diaper. Now, I've seen diaper commercials, movies where people change diapers, and watched my wife change a diaper numerous times right in front of me. I knew it wasn't rocket science. Also, on the plus side, I understood the concept of tape and was aware that the dirty diaper goes away and the clean diaper takes its place. So what the hell was wrong with me?

Invariably, I would place the diaper both upside down and backward underneath Riley. Then, when I found the tape (even though I was pretty sure it was in the wrong location), I would tug at the two little strips until they ripped completely off of the diaper.

One time in the midst of this process, Riley decided to, you know, *go*. Lucky for me it was two in the morning. I was half asleep and had just fed Riley while Lydia was sleeping a much-deserved sleep. I went through my usual routine, and just as I was standing there, bent over, holding my two little pieces of tape while Riley and the diaper remained on the bed, my spider-sense started tingling. I looked down just in time to see a trajectory of liquid baby poo heading right for my face. I suddenly realized I was doing Matrix moves—moves I never thought my body could make: bending completely backward while this brown stream passed centimeters over my head. I decided to take control of the situation by letting out the most womanly scream I could muster.

Waking to the thought that I had dropped the baby, Lydia sat bolt upright in bed, ready to rush to Riley. Then she saw me bent backward, still holding ripped pieces of diaper, and Riley's business covering the wall and floor.

"Oh," she said with a yawn and went back to sleep.

———•———

The Journey

And so begins the journey of fatherhood. It's an exciting, scary, and wonderful ride thus far. I think Riley's going to end up OK, but something tells me it's not the last time I'll be shat upon.

CHAPTER 6

SIBLING REVELRY

When my parents tell stories about me, they will go on and on about what a good child I was. *Nothing* could be further from the truth. I knew good children. My friend Pete who lived down the street was a good child. He dressed up for school, played the violin, was insanely polite to his parents, and had hair parted perfectly down the middle. In fact, the only disagreeable thing I ever heard him say was that he thought the Dallas Cowboys (my favorite football team at the time) were going to lose to the Pittsburgh Steelers in the Super Bowl that year.

Me? I kicked him in the nuts.

The reason my parents believed I was a good child was because of my two older siblings, Jerry and Misty. Jerry just, I don't know, had this knack for getting into trouble. When he was little, he tried to saw a basketball in half so that he could have two. Now forget about the fact he was trying to make two basketballs out of one. Instead, focus on the word *saw*. It's not like my parents left saws lying around next to our Mr. Potato Heads and Atari games. My brother snuck into the garage and climbed the hooks and screws attached to the wall to get the saw. That was his idea of fun.

My sister Misty, on the other hand, was infinitely more subtle. See, Jerry…well, just looking into his eyes made you put your hand on your wallet to make sure it was still there. Misty, on the other hand, looked and acted like the nicest girl you could ever meet. And she was. A very nice girl who would sneak out of the house on a routine basis to party. My bedroom was on the second floor, and right outside my window was the roof of the back porch. I remember one night feeling my bed move, and I woke up to Misty standing on it, opening my window.

"Hey, Jimmy," she whispered. "Don't tell Mom or Dad." And then she vanished like Batman into the shadows. She would actually climb down the railings to the back porch and then hightail it out of there. This went on for a year.

I never told on her. I guess I should have. I mean, this was the girl who would invite her friends over for no other reason than to torment me. They would hold me down while Misty did things to amuse them like—oh, you know—force me to eat fish food. I thought for sure as I gagged and cried that it would appease them, but apparently it wasn't entertaining enough, and soon I was swallowing glitter.

The worst, though, is when Jerry and Misty would fight each other. They were like Ali and Frazier—ruthless, cunning, and deadly. One time, they were babysitting me and somehow got into it. I don't remember how it started, but I do remember Misty dumping some very hot mashed potatoes on Jerry's arm, which immediately started to bubble and boil. Outraged, he growled and snarled and then took chase. Misty, before darting out of the kitchen, grabbed the first thing she could for protection: a discarded banana peel out of the trash. As she turned the corner past the dining room, she came to an immediate halt. Jerry instantly followed with red eyes and hands outstretched and *thwack*! I will never forget that sound of the banana peel slapping my brother's face. Time froze. Misty stood wide-eyed, still holding on to her limp weapon. Then she dropped it and wisely locked herself in the bathroom.

I was sitting on the couch in the living room transfixed, as if I was watching a movie and was lucky enough to know the stars personally. Jerry screamed, and I thought for sure he was suddenly going to grow, turn green, and end up wearing nothing but ripped purple pants. He charged the bathroom door, kicking, punching, slapping, and swearing. I could hear the door creak. Then crack. Then break. Then our parents came home. All they could see was Jerry with a burned arm, a welt on his face, and his foot through the bathroom door. My mom said, "Not again."

Another time Jerry stole our car. Well, I guess he "borrowed" it.

My dad was taking my younger sister, Sherri, and I to a hockey game. It was a work-related event, so my dad had to meet all his coworkers and their kids at a parking lot in downtown Steubenville, Ohio, and then we'd all take a bus to Pittsburgh. So that's what we did. And we enjoyed the hockey game very much, and when we got back to the parking lot, our car was gone. It had vanished. It was as if it had never been there. After my dad went through the classic thought process of *I did park in this lot, didn't I? We did drive here, right? We do own a car, yes?* he came to the conclusion that someone had stolen our poor Dodge Omni. We got a ride to the police station and filed a report.

We were sitting in the police station when my dad suddenly got a look on his face like he had just solved a puzzling mystery. He went to the payphone and called my mom.

"Rachel, check and see if the spare keys are hanging in the garage. Yes, I *do* think. Uh-huh. Of course." He slammed the phone down. "Goddammit!"

We got a police ride back to the parking lot, where the Omni sat, exactly as we had left it. It was the only car in the lot now. My dad thanked the officer, said we wouldn't be filing a complaint just yet, and we got in the car and headed back home to the sound of "That Jerry, I'm going to kill that kid."

As we drove up the highway, we spotted my brother and two of his friends (one of whom was in a cast and using crutches) walking along the side of the road. My dad immediately whipped the car onto the shoulder, squealing the tires as if it were the General Lee, and slammed on the brakes. My brother and his friends stopped dead in their tracks. It was just now turning dark, and I could barely make them out through the car window. The sky was a vibrant navy blue, and the streetlight over their heads made them look like old movie gangsters. It was a very romantic image that lasted about 0.9 seconds.

My dad jumped out of the car and started running toward them. Jerry jumped on the fence beside him and began to climb. His friends followed suit. The one kid threw his crutches over, and then up he went as if he had gotten a special fence-climbing cast just in case something like this happened. They disappeared into the woods, and my dad (who took a little longer to get over the fence) was soon gone as well.

My little sister and I were sitting in our car on the side of the highway alone. The door on the driver's side was still open, and it was officially dark now. I reached over and closed my dad's door, and Sherri and I just hung out for a while. We weren't scared, surprised, or even terribly concerned. At that young age, we had accepted that this is how it worked. Jerry screwed up. My dad got mad. Usually, a chase ensued.

After what felt like an hour but was probably more like, well, I guess it was an hour, we saw my dad struggling back over the fence alone, defeated. He was walking now, slowly, and when he opened the car door and got in, we noticed he was panting heavily and sweating.

He didn't say a word, and the silence felt interminable until finally, Sherri, with all the tact she could muster, leaned forward from the backseat and said, "D'ja get him, Dad? D'ja get him?"

My dad answered the question with a sigh, and we headed for home. "That Jerry," he said after a short while. "I'm gonna kill that kid."

Now, I could start to tell you all the rotten things I did as a kid, but why would I? They would only pale in comparison to the shenanigans of my older siblings. And for that, I love them. Because even after all the crap I pulled, my parents will always tell stories about what a good child I was. Thank you, Jerry. Thank you, Misty. I don't think I say that nearly enough.

CHAPTER 7

WHAT'S BOBBY BROWN'S NAME AGAIN?

OK, if you know me, you know that this is something that has bothered me for a long time. What is Bobby Brown's obsession with his own name? For those of you who don't know who Bobby Brown is, I envy you. God, how I envy you. Anyway, before Bobby Brown became a slow-motion car crash of a life covered by the tabloids and gossip sites, he was the old New Edition kid who went on to have a string of crappy pop tunes in the late '80s. And in almost every one of these crappy pop tunes, he mentions his name. I mean, this guy *really* wants to make sure you know what it is. It's Bobby. Brown.

It starts off kind of subtle, really. In the song (can we really call it that?) cleverly entitled "Humpin' Around," he lets us know, "My name is Brown, that's what I'm called." OK. Got it. No big deal, really. I mean, I already knew his name was Brown, but little reminders never hurt anyone. (If you actually have been hurt by a little reminder, I apologize for misspeaking.)

Then we move to the more popular "Don't Be Cruel," in which he states, "to be with me, Bobby B." OK, so he's using the first letter of his last name to represent his last name (which, if you missed it before, is Brown). I won't fault him for that. He also tells the girl to whom he's singing, "Now you know my name." Now, if she didn't know his name before, that means she never really knew him, and that means he's acting like a psycho stalker, and she has every right to be cruel.

OK, you're thinking, *Yeah, he's a little weird about his name. So what?* Well, that brings us to the song "Every Little Step." Forget the fact that he dresses like Olivia Newton-John in the video and basically does the Electric Slide the entire time. Instead, let's focus on the "rap" section of the song (and I apologize to Mr. Ice Cube for using the word "rap" to describe what Mr. Brown does here). Right away, he gives us an order. He tells us, "When I'm on the mic, don't you dare call me Freddy."

Now, I wasn't going to call him Freddy, were you? Was anybody? Does he have some nemesis who knows his weakness, his Kryptonite, which is being called Freddy while he's on the mic?

We don't have time in the song to ponder this too much because he then goes right into "My name is Brown." So we're forgetting the first name here and going for the tougher-sounding moniker of the last name (like MacGyver or Garfunkel). But wait. He then goes immediately to "That's what they call me." So they call you by your name? Good. But wait. In case you're a little slow, he draws it out for you.

"Brooooooooowwwwwwwwwwwwwwwnnnnnnnnnnnnnnn."

It's so nice of Bobby to help people who can't say words learn his last name. All right, so now I think the guy has a serious issue with people learning his name. But I figure he made his point. Imagine my consternation, then, when he ends the rap with "My name is Bobby, not Uncle Sam." So it's *not* Uncle Sam? Or Freddy? Can I call you Freddy when you're *not* on the mic? So many questions. But I do know this. His name is Bobby. Bobby B. Brown. Brooooooooowwwwwwwwwwwwwwwnnnnnnnnn. And that's what I'll call him.

Oh, well, I guess the only thing worse than Bobby Brown obsessing over his name is obsessing over Bobby Brown obsessing over his name. But I can do what I wanna do. It's my prerogative.

CHAPTER 8

THESE ARE MY THOUGHTS, AND YOU CAN'T HAVE THEM! (SO HERE THEY ARE): PART 2

- I recently saw the movies *Inception* and *Shutter Island*. I guess chances are if you're a dead dream-wife, Leonardo DiCaprio is having trouble letting you go.
- When you think about it, the first person who said "There's more than one way to skin a cat" probably had some real issues.
- Idea: Overweight stand-up comedians compete on a reality TV show where they have to lose weight in a "funny" way. Call it *Laugh Your Ass Off*.
- Can you mow anything besides grass?

- *The Passion of Christ* seems to be somewhat less racist and misogynistic than the passion of Mel Gibson.
- I wonder what the faults were with Preparations A through G.
- Forget the Ouija; I'm inventing a Nonnein board game that allows you to talk to people who are alive.
- Fried eggplant isn't so much heaven in my mouth as it is fried eggplant.
- If there really are fifty ways to leave your lover, why does Paul Simon just keep repeating the same six?
- Elevators are fun but lack the immediate danger that love on an escalator has.
- New studies show that turning a frown upside down results in creepy, upside down frowns, not smiles. Please no longer suggest this to people.
- Killing two birds with one stone isn't just difficult; it's also kind of mean.
- There's Shania, and there's Mark. And ne'er the Twain shall meet.
- I like to throw my arms in the air and wave them like I actually do care a little.
- Idea: Hulked on Phonics. It exposes kids to an overdose of grammar radiation.
- *Annie Get Your Gun* is sadly *not* the sequel to *Annie*. Don't make the same mistake I did.
- I watched *Porky's* on network TV without all the R-rated stuff and finally saw it as the sweet coming-of-age story it was meant to be. Enjoyed all eleven minutes of it.
- *BJ and the Bear* has a totally different meaning today than it did in 1978.
- True, I've never timed it, but every time someone starts with "quick question…" the question seems to take the same amount of time as a normal one.
- My biggest issue with the Internet age is that I somehow know who Amanda Bynes is.
- Reasons why the lady is a tramp, according to Frank Sinatra: (1) Wants to eat dinner before eight o'clock; (2) Likes the theater and is on time to it; (3) Never bothers with people she hates; (4) Doesn't play craps with rich or poor people; (5) Likes the wind in her hair; (6) Doesn't have any money; (7) Hates California; (8) Won't gossip with "the rest of the broads." She sounds awesome. Learn to appreciate an independent woman and stop all the name-calling, OK, pal?

CHAPTER 9

IT'S A BIRD! IT'S A PLANE! IT'S THAT DUMB-ASS KID!

As a kid, I devoured comic books. Not literally, of course. I mean there was that one Wonder Woman comic I put my mouth on, but that's as close as I've come to *eating* a comic book. No, what I meant was that I would read them. A lot.

My mom worked at the corner store, so I would get a discount on the comics that came in every week. My friend Jamie and I would buy them with our paper-route money and then climb the tree in front of his grandma's house, sit in our spots, and read. Then we would trade and read each other's. Then we would reread our own again, both convinced that the one we owned was the better purchase.

I was obsessed with superheroes. In the second grade, I played a pilgrim in the school play and decided that I looked like Zorro in my hat. The day after the play, I snuck my hat in my backpack along with a black mask I made by cutting eyeholes in my sister's scarf. On my short walk from the bus to the school building that morning, I picked up a stick in the yard. I proceeded to the bathroom, took out my hat and mask, and slowly, sensuously, put them on. I looked in the mirror. I was majestic. I branded my stick, cutting a quick Z in the air. Then I walked to the classroom and sat down.

My teacher, Miss Harmon, stared at me for a minute.

"Jimmy, what are you supposed to be?" she asked.

"Zorro," I answered, completely sincere.

A moment of silence followed. Then she just started teaching. The whole day went by, and I was Zorro. It was awesome.

The next day at school, I was Zorro.

The day after that, Zorro.

The day after that, she asked to talk to me.

"Jimmy, um, are you planning on wearing that every day?" she asked.

"Yes," I replied.

"Oh. Well, I just don't feel comfortable with you bringing a big stick into my classroom," she said.

"It's only 'cause I don't have a sword," I explained.

"Ah."

Nothing further was said. But when I got home, my mom told me that Miss Harmon had called her and that I was no longer going to be Zorro at school. I started immediately thinking of which costumed avenger I *was* going to be. My mom, picking up on my thought pattern, clarified that I would be going to school as Jimmy and only Jimmy. Not Jimmy-Man or Super Jimmy. Just Jimmy.

Since the school had suddenly implemented a no-costumed-avengers policy (although I found the loophole and wore my invisible cloak of doom), I focused my attention on my neighborhood.

Home from school, I dashed immediately to my secret hideout (a.k.a. the garage). I found a pair of swimming goggles. I put them on. I saw my older sister's puffy silver moon boots. I put them on (being sure to tuck the bottoms of my black sweatpants in). Work gloves. I put them on. I was wearing a black hoodie, and I pulled my hood over my head. I grabbed some red tarp from my dad's workbench and tied it around my neck like a cape. I took a deep breath. I was ready. They would never know who I was.

I climbed on my easily recognizable purple Huffy bike with the banana seat and headed out. A few blocks up, a man was cutting his grass. He saw me and stopped, the lawnmower going from a growl to complete silence as if in awe.

"Who are you supposed to be, Spider-Man?" he asked me.

I scoffed. I was about to explain that Spider-Man wasn't real and, more importantly, didn't wear a cape, but then suddenly it dawned on me. I had set off to protect the neighborhood without even thinking of my superhero moniker. Since I was in Steubenville, my first thought was Steuben-Man. However, since many people make fun of my hometown by calling it Stupidville, then they would probably…

"You know, it's a little early for Halloween," the man said, interrupting my thoughts.

I said something about keeping himself safe, called him "citizen," and then was back on patrol. On the next street, I drove past the home of a friend of my older brother and sister's. My older brother and sister and their friend were out on the front porch. They were staring superintensely at something, so I stopped my bike to figure out what it was. It was me.

"Is that your brother?" their friend asked.

"No!" both my siblings said instantly and passionately.

I smiled. They were keeping my secret identity. I gave them a friendly wave. On I rode.

Ten minutes later, my mom drove past me. The car came to a screeching halt.

"Get home. Now," she said.

Apparently, my older siblings, instead of being thankful I was out fighting crime in our neighborhood, were somehow rather embarrassed by my antics. They had immediately run home and told my parents that they needed to get me home and out of that stupid outfit before I totally humiliated them.

And that was the end of Steuben-Man. Although it's said that Stupid-Man still lives on.

Now you can laugh all you want, and I have no way to prove it, but I'm still willing to bet that April 11, 1979, was the safest day in our neighborhood.

CHAPTER 10

TWO DAYS AWAY FROM JESUS

My birthday is two days before Christmas. People hear that, and they're like, "Oh, man." You know, like every time I get carded, the guy looks down at my birthday and says, "December twenty-third? Shit, that must have sucked when you were a kid."

You know what? It did. It really sucked because I never got a birthday present. I got one of my Christmas presents two days early. My birthday presents were always wrapped with Christmas wrapping paper. Hell, sometimes they were signed from Santa. Santa doesn't give you birthday presents. Santa gives you Christmas presents!

Then my little sister was born. Two days *after* Christmas. And I can't help thinking, now that I'm older, that my parents could have planned their, you know, adult stuff a little better. But at least I now had someone in my camp. I got a Christmas gift two days early; she got one two days late.

Not too long ago, I was looking through old photographs, and I saw a picture—I would never have remembered this if not for that damn picture, but one year my parents were feeling extremely lazy, I guess, because they decided to celebrate both my sister's and my birthday *on* Christmas day. There's a picture of us both sitting in front of a big chocolate cake. That's *one* cake, mind you. My candles were grouped together on one side of the cake, her candles were on the other side, and in the middle, in pretty pink frosting, it said, "Happy Birthday, Jesus."

Now, my name isn't Jesus. My sister's name isn't Jesus. So not only did we get screwed big time as far as presents go that year, we didn't even get credit for having the damn birthdays.

But I remember being that little kid and thinking that if my mom could have waited two days to give birth to me, if she could have left me in there for two more days, *I* would have been Jesus. Hey, I was a little kid. But it really messed me up. I started really thinking about that, you know? Two days away from Jesus. And, man, being Jesus would've been so cool. Then not only would that kid Eddie have stopped picking on me, but he'd bow down and ask for my forgiveness. And I wouldn't give it to him.

I started walking like Jesus. I'd walk around my room and heal the sick or raise the dead. And say things like "Lo."

I tried to perform miracles. When my pencil would fall off my desk at school, I'd close my eyes and pray for it to be back on my desk. Then I'd slowly open my eyes and see that it was there, resting in the pencil groove, and I'd smile triumphantly. Now, deep down, I knew that Mike, the boy who sat next to me, had reached down and put it back on my desk, but that was deep down. As far as I was concerned, it was my Jesus powers, which kinda resembled the force from *Star Wars*.

So I decided that if my parents celebrated my birthday on Christmas again, and the cake said "Happy Birthday, Jesus" again, then it must be true. I really was Jesus! So you can imagine how disappointed I was when, on the twenty-third of December, my parents decided to throw me a surprise birthday party at Burger King. I remember opening up all my presents and just kind of sitting there pouting. My mom frowned and said, "What's the matter? Didn't you get what you wanted?" I sat there for a second feeling the curious eyes of my friends all over me. Then I just blurted out, "If you could've just waited two more days to have me, I would have been Jesus!"

No one knew what to say. My friends were all staring at me with their mouths hanging open, like I just said a bad word or something. Suddenly I wanted to take the words back or go back in time and say something clever instead or erase the memory from all of their minds or send myself far, far away from everybody. But I knew that I couldn't, that I was always going to be two days away from having that kind of power.

CHAPTER 11

MY DEAREST LYDIA

How exciting that I found some old secret-admirer letters I gave to Lydia all those years ago. Now you'll understand why she fell for me.

A Secret-Admirer Letter to Lydia

My Dearest Lydia,

As I sit here at my computer with my "father" (not sure why I put him in quotes—he really is my father) snoring like a hippo with asthma in the background, I can't help thinking of you. Maybe it's the 317 photographs of you hanging on the wall here or the way I doodle your name on papers all over this desk or the poems I've written to you saved on my hard drive. I don't know. Whatever it is, I can't get you out of my head.

You are like sunshine in a world of rain. You are like a rainbow in a world of...what used to be rain. You are like butter in a world of something that desperately needs butter in order to be happy. I hope this letter doesn't, as you kids say, "freak you out," but I feel like if I never tell you about my feelings, then my feelings will have gone never told to you by me.

Did you ever take chemistry in school? Me neither, but I like to think I know a little bit about it. I believe we have said chemistry. Now I know that some chemistry blows things up, but I think we have the good kind of chemistry.

I'm sorry if this letter isn't making much sense, but I just had a wine cooler and wheeeeeeee! Know what I mean? Of course you do; that's what I like about you. That and the way you chew gum.

If you are interested in knowing who I am, please meet me at the Empire State Building on New Year's Eve at midnight. Try not to get hit by a car.

Shit, I dropped my pencil. I guess it doesn't really matter since I'm typing this. Oh, well. I'd best go now as some strange men just walked by me carrying my television.

Your secret admirer,
~~Jimmy Mak~~ (oops)
JM← (clue)

Another Secret-Admirer Letter to Lydia

My Dearest Lydia,

I heard it through the grapevine that you are sick. *Heard it through the grapevine* is not just an expression—I have a real enchanted grapevine planted in my love garden that tells me things! You *must* come over and see it sometime. (Bring red wine.)

Anywhos, I thought I'd send you this poem to make you feel better. If you like it, please tape a pink cutout paper heart on your living room window tonight. If you don't have any pink cutout paper hearts, they sell them at Michael's Arts and Crafts. If you don't like my poem, well, no offense, but that means you don't understand poetry. (That's OK; sometimes being dumb is endearing. Example: Boner from *Growing Pains*.)

Here you go:

A Poem to Make Lydia Feel Better

In this land of winter and ice
Sometimes our hearts catch cold
They yearn for what they cannot have
And get pneumonia (sp?) of the soul

Let my love be the chicken soup you put in your mouth
Let my care be your afghan so warm
Let my breath be the good-smelling kind on your neck
Let my umbrella keep you dry in the storm

Tho' you ne'ermore stand atop the mount'ain
Or o'er the misty springs thy talisman
Besieged a fodder for a fount'ain
'Ere kings go blindly and prod poor Palice men

Fine

Does that make you feel better? I sure hope so. If not, maybe try some cold medicine. (I think Advil works pretty well.) I must go now because somebody (my dad) is getting home from work and will need the computer to eBay. Boooooring. Take care,

PS: OK, confession time. I stole the third verse of my poem from Geoffrey Chaucer. I didn't mean to; it just fit so perfectly! I'm not a bad person! (Unless…)

Yet Another Secret-Admirer Letter to Lydia

My Dearest Lydia,

Sorry I haven't corresponded in so long, but I needed some space. So I went to the NASA Museum. I highly recommend it. Outer space. Crazy, huh? Hey, if you owned a galaxy, I'd visit your black hole. Ha-ha. That's a joke. Maybe you can use that if you ever become a stand-up? If you do use it, I may ask for a little compensation but not much. "Compensation" means money.

I'm wearing a robe right now.

So, anyway, what's your favorite color? Mine's the same as yours.

Holy moly!

Sorry, but MTV's on in the background, and some rappist just thrust his thingie at the camera. Maybe I'm just old fashioned, but what was so wrong with the horse and buggy, know'msayin'?

I can't wait for us to meet. I would love to tell you about my childhood. Or I can tell you about my cousin's childhood. It's actually way better than mine.

Are you *so* curious as to who I am? A lot of people are. Can you say "identity theft?" (Ha-ha—another joke. You can't use that one.)

Ciao!
Me

No doubt thanks to my wordcraft, Lydia and I have been married for over fifteen years now. I'd show you the other 327 letters I wrote her, but to be honest…they're a little weird.

CHAPTER 12

THESE ARE MY THOUGHTS, AND YOU CAN'T HAVE THEM! (SO HERE THEY ARE): PART 3

- Hard to believe it's been over thirty years since that woman blinded that dude with science.
- I'm writing *Click Bait*, the movie. It starts out being a normal movie about social-media websites that promote a silly sentence to get people to look at their pages, but you won't believe what happens next. Check out www.clickbaitthemovie.com.
- I just got a degree in reverse psychology! And my parents said I'd never do it.

- I can't believe when Elvis was recording "Are You Lonesome Tonight" and got to the line where he says, "You know, someone said all the world's a stage" that no one in the studio had the balls to scream, "It was Shakespeare! Shakespeare said it! Everyone knows that! Yes, you are the king…of idiots!"
- I'm betting these days the singer Rockwell never feels like somebody's watching him.
- I overheard a commercial on the radio that said, "At Burger King, we know that size does matter." Sounds like it may be harder to get a job there now compared to when I was a kid.
- Turns out "get out of my dreams, get into my car" is a terrible first thing to say to a woman. Thanks a lot, Billy Ocean.
- Still can't believe my idea for "illiterature, books for people who can't read or write by people who can't read or write," has never caught on.
- I keep waiting for the Go-Bots movie to come out. I assume it will be similar to the Transformers movie, only it will be cheaper and blander and will fall apart after an hour.
- Say all you want about the '80s, but in my opinion, it was the only decade to really tackle the arm-wrestling genre in cinema.
- People who use obscure literary references unnecessarily make me wanna go all Rodion Romanovich Raskolnikov on 'em.
- Definition of the word *grease* (according to the Frankie Valli Dictionary): GREASE: (n, v, adj): (1) The word, as in the word that you heard. (2) Containing both groove and meaning. (3) The time. (4) The place. (5) The motion. (6) The way we are feeling. (7) How some people misspell *Greece*.
- If there's ever another scandal in the Watergate Hotel, would it now have to be called Watergate-gate?
- I think the most challenging thing in the world would be if you were a method actor and had to play Daniel Day Lewis in a movie.
- Even after all this time, my friend just passed the dutchie from the *right*-hand side. Idiot.
- I can't help but wonder if the first person who was told to stop beating a dead horse was, in fact, beating a dead horse.
- If Bo, Luke, and Daisy were all cousins, and Jesse was an uncle to all three of them, that means Jesse had three siblings who all had one child. And all three of those kids ended up living with their childless uncle. However way you look at it, something really messed up happened with that family.
- I think the person I feel sorry for the most is the kid who really does have a girlfriend in Canada.

- I imagine soon conversations in school will go like this:
  History teacher: What caused the civil war?
  Student: Iron Man thought the government should keep tabs on the superheroes, and Captain America disagreed.
- People who say all my references are dated can kiss my grits.

II. SOMEWHAT SERIOUS

CHAPTER 13

SEPTEMBER 11, 2001

I was supposed to be at work at 8:30am for a meeting, a meeting I had called, a meeting I was in charge of, a meeting I had completely forgotten about. I sauntered into the office at 9:00am and casually headed to my desk. My fellow manager immediately gave me grief about the meeting and how this kind of thing simply cannot happen. "Shit!" Not a good way to start the morning.

At 9:15am, I was hard at work, a little depressed that people had come in early counting on me and I had let them down. Suddenly, I heard some talk outside the office of a plane that had hit one of the twin towers at the World Trade Center. I immediately thought, *Jesus, that sucks* but thought of it in the same way I would about a car crash I heard about on the news. I couldn't believe I missed that stupid meeting. I kept working.

Someone suddenly called out, "Hey, man, you should come listen to this." I walked out of my office and saw staff members sitting there, listening to the radio. Another plane had hit the other tower. Then we heard that a plane hit the Pentagon. Then a plane crashed outside of Pittsburgh, Pennsylvania. My eyes started darting back and forth. What the hell? We…we were under attack. Today. No warning. I caught myself looking up for no reason. What the hell was going on? One of the towers collapsed. Then the other one. People dead. Twin towers gone. We all just…just sat there. Impotent.

I expected the attacks to go on all day, but they didn't. Four planes. The rest were accounted for. Hours went by. It was over.

My wife and I work together, and at about three in the afternoon, we took a walk outside just to get away from the madness. We walked to one of the benches that outlined a ground-level fountain in the center of town. The fountain was a large square in shape, and it spurted out water randomly at different places. Parents would bring their children there in bathing suits and let them play, but that day it was empty except for one older gentleman, easily in his late sixties, walking a little girl who looked to be about three through the fountain. Every time the water spurted, the little girl laugh-screamed, and the older man quickened his step until they were safe outside the square. Then they would turn around and head back toward the danger, he walking right behind her, she reaching up and holding his fingers so as not to fall.

My wife closed her body into mine and rested her head on my shoulder. The sky was a perfect blue, dark and bright at the same time—a comic-book blue. And the yellows and reds and greens of the surrounding buildings made everything a cartoon. Trees rustled peacefully, and I closed my eyes, listening to the sounds of water splashing and a small girl laughing, and with my wife in my arms, I thought, *Everything in my life is perfect.*

Then I heard a new sound, and when I opened my eyes, I saw a plane in the sky, and my heart started beating faster, and I froze, watching the white streak stretch across the sky, and sadness overwhelmed me because I knew. It was all different now. Everything was different.

CHAPTER 14

PLEASE
(A MOMENT IN TIME AT THE GROCERY STORE THAT STUCK WITH ME)

He was just an old man, a stranger standing in front of me in line at the grocery store, but I immediately felt drawn to him. I wanted to sit with him at a bar and listen to his life story. I couldn't help but stare.

His sagging face was weathered with life. He looked down mostly, but when he bravely looked up for moments at a time, it was as if his eyes had to cut through memories of loss: a dead wife, a runaway daughter, a missed fortune. He was wearing a T-shirt sporting a cartoon man with frazzled hair on a surfboard. His pants were silver and dressy, and his shoes were shiny black. As he dug into his wallet for money, his left knee jerked in and out, perhaps moving to the beat of a song he remembered from long ago.

The checkout girl looked for a short time at the two cartons of Basic 100s cigarettes, which were separated a little from his other purchases.

"These yours?" she asked him.

"Please," he replied softly, sadly.

"Payin' with cash?"

"Please."

She took his money before he finished handing it to her as if she was afraid he'd change his mind, and he stood there for a second still holding on to his invisible dollars. Then he sighed, and his embarrassed hand searched for shelter in his pocket, only to spring to life once again to catch the few coins she was dropping.

Suddenly, he turned to me, perhaps feeling my stare, my fascination. He looked fully at me, his eyes no longer squinting, and he gave me a wink. I smiled self-consciously, and he turned back, picked up his white plastic bundles of treasure, and headed back to his life of cigarettes and pepperoni sticks, his leg still moving to surfing songs of his youth.

I think of him from time to time at odd moments: in the middle of arguing with my wife or when I'm completely engrossed in a good film. And I think about his wink and whether it was a warning or a welcome, perhaps letting me in on the secret that one day you wake up and all you can say is "please."

CHAPTER 15

NO TROUBLE IN LITTLE CHINA:
MY ADVENTURE IN HONG KONG

My wife, Lydia, and I were about to celebrate our fourteenth anniversary, which is the ivory anniversary. Yeah, don't think that ivory anniversaries go over the way they used to.

"My love for you is as big as a dead elephant. Here's a tusk."

We had been talking for a while about going overseas for our vacation. Ireland? Italy? Then I thought about our friend Mike, who moved to Hong Kong eight years ago. Asia? Hmmm, I knew more about the band than I did the continent. We contacted Mike and gave him the dates we were thinking about.

"That's perfect for me! I'm a great tour guide! Come visit!" (He's a very loud Facebooker.) We went out for Chinese to talk it over. My wife asked her fortune cookie "Should we go visit Mike in Hong Kong?" She opened the cookie and read the little paper: "Buy that ticket takes that special trip." Although not grammatically correct, we caught the gist.

Passports were obtained. Childcare was planned (thank God for grandparents). Neck pillows were bought. We boarded a plane in Columbus at 7:20 Monday morning. An hour and a half later, we switched planes in Toronto and flew fifteen hours straight to Hong Kong. We flew into…the future (dun dun duuuuunnn). Hong Kong is exactly twelve hours ahead of Columbus, so even though it felt like we arrived at 2:30 Tuesday morning, it turned out it was 2:30 Tuesday afternoon. I kept telling my body that time was a manmade construct. My body kept telling me to fuck off.

Mike picked us up at the airport. We rode the train back to Hong Kong Island and then caught the ferry to Lamma Island. This is where he lived and where we would be staying. Lamma Island has a cool, artsy vibe to it. We walked around the island, taking in the various little shops and markets. We walked into a little store called Brothers, and each of us bought a beer to drink while we walked around. Open container is 100 percent OK in Hong Kong. I was going to like this place.

We hung out on the beach for a bit. We visited Mike's house, played with his puppy, ate a crazy-good mango, and then went to dinner. They don't give you napkins in the restaurants in China. And since napkin means "diaper" there, I guess it's a good thing.

After dinner, Lydia and I were barely awake, so we said good-bye to our friend and went back to our room. The room we were staying in was like a little apartment above a restaurant. It had a patio that faced the ocean. Oh, and it was owned by the actor Chow Yun-Fat's parents. I asked Lydia if she wanted to play *Crouching Tiger, Hidden Dragon*. She said no. We were asleep by 8:30 p.m.

———————

Wednesday

I woke up at midnight, and my body said, "It's noon. Get out of bed. Let's go!" I forced myself to go back to sleep. At 3:00 a.m., my body said, "Come on, man. What's your problem? It's time to move!" I told my body to fuck off. We were even.

We met Mike at 8:30am and took the half-hour ferry ride to Hong Kong Island. Then we took the train to Sha Tin and met up with Christopher, another friend who had moved to Hong Kong. The four of us then trekked up a mountain to see the Temple of Ten Thousand Buddhas.

The temple is beautiful. On your way up the many, many, many (many) steps, there are a number of large, golden Buddhas in various positions and with various facial expressions—some praying, some screaming, some with arms coming out of their eyeballs.

It's kind of a MacGuffin. (Hitchcock term. Look it up.) You think these are the ten thousand Buddhas, but they're not. Once you reach the top and enter the temple, you really see them—ten thousand small Buddhas that line the inside walls of the temple from floor to ceiling. It's hard to describe, and there was no photography allowed, but it was quite overwhelming and extremely beautiful.

We headed back down and had lunch at an authentic Chinese restaurant. No orange chicken, no General Tso's, and no fortune cookies can be found in these places. I got spicy beef and rice (simple enough), and it was delicious. I also decided that starting then and there, I would eat my meals with chopsticks. Lunch lasted seven hours. (Slight exaggeration.)

We then went to Jordan to walk around the Temple Street night market. Lydia bought a painting of Hong Kong from one of the merchants—assuming he was the artist, she even tipped him (which he was clearly not used to). We ended up seeing the exact same painting at about seven other locations, so it turned out to not be the one-of-a-kind painting she thought it was. We still like it, though: it is special to us, representing a magical night in Hong Kong.

Thursday

On Thursday morning, we took the ferry to Hong Kong Island and then boarded another boat for a day trip to Macau. That's right—we spent our time in another country going to another country. After an hour's boat ride, we were there.

Macau is an interesting place. It was once a Portuguese colony and has a number of Christian seminaries (as well as Buddhist temples like those in China). It has also recently become a gambling mecca with new, fancy-looking casinos everywhere. So I guess it's just your typical Asian-Portuguese-Christian-historic-Vegas-y type place.

We hailed a taxi and asked the driver to take us to one of the seminaries. Mike showed the driver where it was on the map. The man looked utterly confused. Mike pointed to a different seminary. The man still looked confused and just shook his head no. We hailed another taxi. Mike showed him the seminary on the map. The man pointed to a general area and asked a question in Chinese.

"You're asking me?" said Mike. "Yes, it's in that general direction. Not up, not down, but that way somewhere."

We hailed our third taxi, and the driver kinda sorta took us where we wanted to go. I learned that to be a taxi driver in Macau, knowledge of the area is not really requisite.

We visited a number of seminaries and little museums. We visited St. Paul's façade, a giant church that had burned down, leaving only the giant front exterior. We ate a Portuguese egg tart. So. Good.

Later in the day, we hit the casinos: MGM, Wynn, City of Dreams. Aware of our budget, Lydia and I hit the nickel slots. Although the machines' signs boasted a wide variety, they all ended up being the same game. We lost a little bit of money. Mike cleaned up on the poker table. Bastard.

We left Macau a little more broke and a lot more tired. But we did get to see an Asian breakdance battle on the upper floor of one of the casinos. So there was that. And I'm pretty damn sure none of the breakdancers were daddies. Daddies shouldn't breakdance.

———

Friday

We started the day walking through Hong Kong Park. This is like the Central Park of Asia except a lot hillier. They have a very cool aviary there, and we saw a number of interesting birds.

We caught a taxi to Stanley to visit the market there. The markets in Hong Kong are like giant Asian flea markets. They sell everything from clothes to toys to sharkskins (really). They even sell cardboard replicas of things like iPads, cars, and whiskey. I found out that people buy these cardboard replicas, burn them at a temple while praying for someone, and the idea is that the deceased person will receive these items in the afterlife. So you burn a cardboard bottle of Jameson, and then Grampa can keep himself nice and boozed up in heaven. When I die, please burn a cardboard Tom Waits record for me. I'd appreciate it.

After the Stanley market, we took a minibus to Causeway Bay and walked around Hong Kong's Times Square. We jumped on a trolley, affectionately called the "ding ding," and rode through the city.

Mike had a wedding to go to, so he showed us how to get back to the ferry. We should go to this building, go up the escalator, cross the overpass, and go straight. No problem. We said good-bye. We went to the building, up the escalator, and kept going straight. We kept going. And going. We were going up on what we found out was the longest escalator in the world. We kept going up and up. We felt it was weird that Mike hadn't mentioned how long it was going to take. Finally, the escalator came to the end. Nothing looked familiar. I asked someone where the ferry was, and he pointed to the way we had just come from. We had just gone twenty minutes in the wrong direction.

We went back down. Of course, there was no escalator on the way back down—just steps and hills. We ended up back where we started. I realized we were supposed to turn after going up the escalator; that's where we had gone wrong. Mike later said, "You kept going *up* expecting to see the water?" Well, yeah. I mean, we were on the other side of the globe. If toilet water flushes in the opposite direction in some countries, couldn't water be above land? After all, we were in the future! Who knows what's possible?

Or we could just blame our mistake on jetlag.

This was technically our anniversary, so Lydia and I were excited to celebrate. We finally made it back to Lamma Island, and our plan was to check out all the fun little bars on the strip. We had dinner, hit one bar, and couldn't stop yawning. We went back to our room to watch a movie. Again, we were both asleep by 8:30 p.m. Happy anniversary.

Saturday

We took the train to Wan Chai to walk around. We visited a temple and a cool little museum called Hong Kong House of Stories. The woman there played a record of Hong Kong music for me. We walked through a local grocery market. We rode a glass elevator and got a great view of Hong Kong.

We had dim sum for lunch. If you've never had dim sum, I highly recommend it. People push these little carts around with signs on them, and you just tell them what you want, and they give you a little wooden steamer bowl with usually three or four food items.

Things like barbecue rolls, shrimp noodles, and so on. We had mango pudding for dessert. Oh, man. I tried to make this when I got back to the States. It didn't work.

After this, we went "junking" in Soho, looking through a number of art and antique stores. We went to the ladies' market in Mong Kok. I was searching for a coffee cup. Little-known fact—not many people drink coffee in Asia.

At this point, Lydia and Mike decided they wanted foot massages. My lower back was killing me, so I opted for a regular back massage. In Hong Kong, every fifth building is a massage parlor (only a slight exaggeration). Christopher had warned us a couple days before that the ones with smiley faces on the sign or up a long flight of steps were the "adult" massage parlors, so to speak.

Mike led us into one that had a smiley-face sign *and* was up a long flight of stairs.

"It's fiiiiiine," he said.

I was steered into a small room with a cot in it. On the cot was a pair of shorts made from thick paper. I nervously got undressed and pulled the papery shorts over my under-wear. The woman entered and immediately got to work on my back. She stepped up on the bed and literally walked all over me. It felt really good, actually. My back was feeling better. I knew time had to be almost up, so I relaxed: I was getting a good massage, and that was it. Then she motioned me to turn over. I did so hesitantly. She worked on my legs and then said, "Hey."

I looked at her. She pointed at me with one hand, and the other made the, ahem, jerking-off motion. "Yeah?" she asked.

"No," I said.

"No?" she asked, totally confused. I don't think she heard no very often. She shrugged her shoulders, waved, and left. I realized I had tensed up so much that I pretty much undid all of the massage work she had done.

We left the Handy House and headed back to Wan Chai to bar hop. A lot of beer, a lot of live music, and a lot of laughter. A really fun night.

Sunday

A little hungover. We ate breakfast at McDonald's. Yes, McDonald's. Say what you want, still the best hangover food on the planet. We gave Mike grief because he had told us he would take us to Monkey Mountain, but that had fallen off the agenda.

"We want to see monkeys, dammit!" we screamed at him.

So he decided to take us to Pineapple Dam Park at the Shing Mun reservoir for a little walk in the woods. We took a minibus to the park. Lydia and I were still a little worse for wear. We got off the bus and saw a bunch of steps that led up to the park. I immediately began complaining about the climb. We got to the top of the steps and followed Mike down one of the paths.

We saw them. We saw the monkeys! There were signs that said not to look them in the eyes; they saw that as a challenge and would attack you. These monkeys don't mess around.

After a half hour, I realized we had been walking nonstop up a mountain.

"Where are you taking us?" I asked.

"Just a little trek around the reservoir," he replied.

An hour later, we stopped to rest.

"I got some good news," said Mike, looking at a sign. "We're about halfway there."

I think Lydia started to cry.

"Maybe you'll see another monkey?" he suggested hopefully.

"It's probably better if you don't talk," I whispered.

After the third hour hiking this magical mountain that seemed to go only up, I had a brilliant idea. The next monkey I saw, I would stare him in the eyes until he killed me.

We finished the nearly four-hour "little walk in the woods" and were ready to collapse.

There was only one thing to do—more foot massages. I stayed out of any private rooms and paper shorts this time.

We met Christopher at Hong Kong Island and caught the tram to the peak. The view of Hong Kong from the peak is awe-inspiring. No picture will do it justice.

While there, we saw a restaurant called Mak's Noodle.

"There's more than one of these in Hong Kong," Mike informed me.

Apparently, my noodle is very popular there.

———

Monday

This was our last full day in Hong Kong. We took a sky lift to Lantau Island to see Big Buddha. This was probably the most touristy thing we did on the trip; it has a very Disneyland feel to it (except, instead of Mickey Mouse, it's a 112-foot-tall Buddha.) There are an enormous number of (you guessed it) stairs that lead to the Buddha. Actually, it's pretty amazing, and inside is a museum that tells the story of Buddha through wonderful artwork.

From there we took a bus to Tai O, a little fishing village about a half hour away. We took a boat ride around the village. The houses are all on stilts in the water, and people go straight from their back door into their little boats. After the boat ride, we walked around on little bridges connecting the village. We had an afternoon beer, which tasted perfect. I tried some squid jerky, which tasted less than perfect.

We took the bus back to Big Buddha, and Mike led us to an area called the Path of Wisdom. This is where he proposed to his wife, Bee. There are giant pillars of wood sticking out of the ground with Chinese poems carved into them. Even though you can't read them, you can't help but be moved. It is simply breathtaking.

We took the sky lift back and met up with Christopher in Tsim Sha Tsui. Christopher wanted us to eat at an Indian place in Chunk King Mansion. On the way to this place, people standing outside their shops aggressively tried to hand us their business cards. They would follow us, scream in our faces, and wave their business cards maniacally. It felt as if they had to hand out all of their business cards or something terrible would happen to their families; it was that kind of desperation.

Chung King Mansion is the most unmansion-like building I've ever been in. It was run-down and shady, and the people inside looked like they were up to no good. We took a tiny elevator up to the seventh floor, where the Indian restaurant was. Mike had to fill out a form to become a member in order for us to eat there. Luckily (and not unsurprisingly), the food was totally worth it.

After dinner, we had a nightcap at a bar called Ned Kelley's Last Stand. It had an Australian theme. A Filipino jazz band was playing some great Cole Porter tunes. At one point, I realized I was drinking Danish beer with my American friends listening to a Filipino jazz band in an Australian-themed bar in China. Not a bad way to end our last night there.

Tuesday

We said our good-byes to Lamma Island, met up with Mike, and rode the ferry for the last time. We had dim sum again for lunch. Mike had to go to Singapore for work, so he once again left us on our own. He was an amazing host and tour guide. Lydia teared up as we watched him go.

We had some time to kill, so just for fun, we got back on the crazy-long escalator we initially got lost on. We popped into a bar and drank our last beer in Hong Kong. We searched the area for a Portuguese egg tart but couldn't find any. We took the train to the airport, boarded a plane, and, after a stressful layover in Toronto, we were home.

Overall, Hong Kong was truly a magnificent place. If you go, I highly recommend the markets, the temples, and the food. Mostly, though, I recommend you have friends who have lived there a number of years. I know that worked out well for us.

Also, stay away from the massage parlors with long flights of stairs and smiley faces on the signs. Or don't. I won't judge.

CHAPTER 16

CONTENT

The other day, my little girl asked me what my favorite number was. She said her favorite number was four, which, interestingly enough, happened to coincide with her age. Well, I'm not sure why, but I immediately flashed back to a night when I was seventeen years old.

It was pretty late, and I wasn't doing much, just watching TV in my rec room. My parents were upstairs, so I decided to get out and take a little walk. There was a Dairy Queen a couple of blocks away, and I walked to it and sat down on the picnic table outside.

It was one of those nights that seem to exist only in memory. You know, the sky was deep blue, and the breeze eased its way past me in waves. The crickets were screaming, and the moon looked like a big, blind eye. Just one of those perfect nights. I don't remember thinking about much, just sitting there mostly, throwing some of the gravel pebbles across the road, but I felt, I don't know, calm maybe.

Content.

I felt content. It was life before work and marriage and kids. I was just a teenager sitting on a picnic table throwing stones.

I don't know why I happened to remember that particular night, but it made me feel good to remember it, and I was just about to tell my little girl that my favorite number was seventeen when my mind let go, and she came into focus again.

She was staring up at me, with her big, blue eyes and some sort of pudding substance clinging to the sides of her mouth. She was wearing her hair Pebbles Flintstone-style, with the one ponytail on top of her head.

"Daddy!" she screamed and pursed her pudding lips and threw her hands, now fists, to her hips. She was getting a little impatient and wanted an answer.

"My favorite number is four," I told her.

And when she gave me the big, open-mouth smile, proudly showing off her two missing teeth (the smile she usually saved for photographs), I knew I had answered correctly.

CHAPTER 17

SHARING SHERRI

I believe in stories. This one is about my sister Sherri.

"Something's wrong with the computer system," the pilot announced. "We've got some technicians looking at it, and we'll hopefully be off the ground real soon."

My dad and I looked at each other and sighed. We were in a plane in Washington, DC, heading to Florida. My heart started beating crazy fast. I just wanted to be in the air. Then

I wondered what, exactly, my hurry was. I mean, after all, I was heading to Florida to watch my younger sister die.

My sister Sherri was two years younger than I was. I was born two days before Christmas, and she was born two days after Christmas. We couldn't be more different. I loved school; she hated it. I loved movies; she thought of Paul Newman as "the salad-dressing guy." I loved Johnny Cash; she…also loved Johnny Cash. I mean, seriously, who doesn't love Johnny Cash? And like most siblings, as we got older, we became friends, got into arguments, didn't talk for a while, and became friends again. And now, after just turning forty-one a couple of weeks ago, she was lying in a hospital room in Florida, taking her final breaths.

We sat, sighed, and squirmed for an hour, and finally the plane took off. When we landed in Florida, we rushed to the hospital. It was midnight. We were met by my mom; my older sister, Misty; my older brother, Jerry, and his wife, Christie. We all went into the room to see Sherri.

Sherri went to the hospital with a severe case of the flu. Then she got double pneumonia and became confused about where she was and what was going on. The doctors were having trouble getting the fluid out of her lungs and put her under sedation. Then she was diagnosed with acute respiratory distress syndrome. Then she had a stroke, and the doctors told us she would never be able to form words again. Then they informed us that she was brain dead, and the ventilator was the only thing keeping her alive. This all happened in the span of a week.

We took turns holding her hand and kissing her forehead. We hugged each other. They removed the ventilator. At 2:08 a.m., she was gone. My baby sister was gone. We all went into the waiting room and told our favorite Sherri stories. I believe in stories.

My sister had gotten us a place to sleep at this giant house near the hospital. It was kind of like a bed and breakfast except the rooms were much more like hotel rooms. In our room, my dad and I were assigned a bed, and my brother and his wife got the bed next to us. Christie said, "Just so you know, I snore." I assured her that was the least of our concerns, and we all nodded off.

An hour later, a noise woke me up. It sounded like the sound that the offspring of a puma and a chainsaw would make. And that baby was loudly devouring a shrieking monkey. Assuming it was my dad, I elbowed him in the ribs.

"It's not me!" he whisper-screamed.

"Jerry's making that noise?" I asked.

"No. Christie."

I couldn't believe that cacophonous caterwauling was coming from my brother's gentle, diminutive wife. But it was. I lay awake wondering if the people in the room next to us were calling the local zoo to see if their African elephant had escaped. Christie and my brother had driven to Florida from Georgia, and I knew they were beat, so I decided not to wake her. I decided to make the best of it. I would try to think of it as white noise cranked up to eleven. Regardless, I would just stay in bed.

"Let's get out of here," said my dad.

"OK," I replied.

We grabbed our pillows, left the room, and went in search of a place to sleep. We went downstairs to the main lounge area, where there was a couch and a big, comfy chair. But as luck would have it, the heater on the first floor wasn't working, and this particular Florida night was freezing. We went back up to the second floor. It was like a scene from a sad *Mission Impossible* episode—my dad and I sneaking through this strange house in the dark, pillows tucked under our arms.

I found a small computer room. There was barely room enough for me on the floor, but it was dark and quiet. I told my dad I was going to crash in there. He said he would go back downstairs and deal with the cold. I threw my pillow on the floor and was figuring out how to contort my body around the desk when my dad ran back around the corner.

"Jimmy!" he screamed. "The Promised Land!"

He led me through a few hallways until we ended up at the second-floor lounge. It was a huge room with a big screen TV and two very comfortable-looking couches. It was beautiful. Without saying a word, we plopped down on our chosen couches and immediately dozed off. It was 5:00 a.m.

At 9:00 a.m., my dad shook me awake, telling me that someone had just walked in, looked at us, and walked back out. Afraid we would somehow get in trouble, we trekked back to our room. Jerry heard us come in and immediately started laughing. Christie was asleep, and the noise, thank God, was gone.

"Christie woke me up a little while ago, telling me you guys were gone," said Jerry. "She felt so bad and kept saying, 'I tried to warn 'em, baby. I tried to warn 'em.'"

"She warned us she snored," I said. "She didn't warn us she was an alien. The correct warning should have been 'Run. Run as far as you can, and don't look back.'"

My brother laughed. Then he laid his head down and nodded off. I closed my eyes as well, hoping for another few hours of sleep. Then the noise started again.

"I'm out," my dad screamed. He grabbed his pillow and split.

I stayed. I thought about the prom show in high school when I danced like Michael Jackson, and when I was done, Sherri screamed out, "That's my brother!" Eventually I fell asleep. Even with the noise.

The next day, we told the rest of the family the story of Christie's snoring and my and my dad's adventuring through the strange wilderness armed with pillows. They laughed until they cried. We told that story the next day and laughed just as hard. I told that story just the other day and still laughed.

That story helped so much. It reminded us of laughter and joy in the face of pain and sorrow. Every time I see Christie, I thank her for having that wonderful snore.

I believe in stories. I believe that stories keep people alive.

And I plan on doing my part to make sure Sherri lives a very long time.

III. SOMEWHAT SAPPY

CHAPTER 18

WE
(WRITTEN FOR MY WIFE AFTER FINDING OUT SHE WAS PREGNANT)

We talked and talked and talked
    And then kissed in the beer tent with jazz music swimming in the air
    And the voice of the crowd becoming a mosquito buzz in our ears
We went to your place and ate ice cream with chocolate magic shell in our boxer shorts
    And stared a little too long at each other between sentences and tried to get sexy but
    laughed when the TV said,
    "*Mr. Belvedere*, weekdays at five."
We moved my things in with your things, and they became our things
    And we, best friends now, learned each other's language
    And I woke up one day surprised to find you confident
    In conversations about Cary Grant movies and comic books
We connected, then disconnected, then knew it was forever at the Ohio State Fair
    When we noticed the little cars that carried you into the haunted house were actually
    smiling snail buggies borrowed from another ride
    The Happy Snails of Death, you said
    For your *slow* descent into hell, I replied
We celebrated my birthday
    Slowly dancing to soft violin music
    Keeping the beat by the car horns pounding outside like my heart
    And it ended with me on one knee and a James Dean smile
We are…you and me
    How funny life will be, then,
    When "we" becomes three.

CHAPTER 19

HARMONICA FAREWELL
(A MEMORY OF THE LAST TIME I SAW MY GRANDMOTHER)

Old lady on the porch,
What are you smiling for?
Don't you know your time is near?
And I fear we'll never see you here again.
And what's that in your hand?
A harmonica. Is your plan
To take one last stand and replace
The creak creaks of your rocker

With some sweet-ass melodies about felonies
Or a life you wish you'd had?
Old lady on the porch,
That sound is so sweet, I tap my feet
So sad, sad, sad, I can't help but smile.
And I'll remember this always,
Hoping there are other days
When I see your crazy-old face
Smiling on the porch,
But knowing, somehow knowing as I'm going
(That sound still ringing like a beautiful bell)
That you're about to die, and you just said good-bye,
A harmonica farewell.

HI, BUTTERFLY

For Riley

It's night, and the light from the television
Is a warm prison for your mother and me
As we let the trials and smiles of the day fade away
And you, my little girl, are curled up in a chair
So comfy lying there, deep in sleep,
When suddenly your arm reaches out, and you happily shout,
"Hi, butterfly!"
Like you're greeting an old friend come to see you again,
But your eyes never open, and in a second it's over.
As your arm comes back down, and your weight shifts around,
You're sound asleep once more,
And we've just eavesdropped on your dream, pretty thing.
And I wonder if you and that butterfly are flying high in the sky
Together, or perhaps it was just passing by
With no time to unwind
But now thinking there's nothing better in the world
Than a smile and a hi from such a pretty young girl.
And your mother touches my hand, and I understand
As we listen to your gentle breathing
That one day you'll be leaving,
Flying away on those colorful wings,
And on that day, your mother and I
Will no doubt cry and sigh
"Good-bye, butterfly."

CHAPTER 21

FATHER, DAUGHTER, MOON

The father stepped outside, holding his daughter.
She had woken up crying (screaming really) from night terrors
Or from a tummy ache
Or from the bullying bars on the crib falsely promising her a life in prison.
Truthfully, he didn't know.
He was half-awake when he picked her up,
And his walk down the stairs had been in slow motion and movie-like
With her scream-sound playing like an angry song.
The father knew to take the daughter outside when she was like this.
She was so young that every time they stepped out of the front door,
A new world magically unfolded before her
(Like a magician who pulls away his kerchief to reveal *everything*),
And, overwhelmed by the beauty and loneliness,
The daughter would instantly fall into silent and humble awe.
This night was no different.
As they stood on the front porch, her shrieks ceased
(Though she was still cry-breathing and damp-cheeked).
The father pointed to the moon,
Endlessly staring down at them.
"Moon," said the father.
The daughter followed the father's arm with her eyes, up past the finger,
Until she locked onto the bright object in the sky.
She looked back at the father, who pointed again.
"Moon," he said.
Once again, her eyes made the arduous journey from her father's finger,
Up through space and past the stars,
Until she saw the moon.
She looked back at her father.
"Where is the moon?" he asked her.

She pointed to it.

Her breathing was now normal, and moonlight was reflected on her tear-stained face.

"Impressive, isn't it?" asked the father.

She continued pointing.

"You know what would be more impressive?" he asked.

She glanced at him.

"If you went back inside and went to sleep. And smile while you sleep.

Because we love you. You are so, so loved."

Then he kissed her on the forehead and took her back inside,

Back to her room,

And laid her down in the crib.

Instantly her eyes closed, and she slept,

Feeling more impressive than the moon.

(And the father would tell you with complete conviction

That, yes, indeed she was.)

CHAPTER 22

THE NIGHT THE MOON BLEW AWAY

For Rosalyn

Holding my youngest daughter, Rosalyn,
on the front porch
at night,
looking for the moon, I asked her,
"I don't see it, do you?"
"It blew away," she replied,
her two-year-old eyes searching the heavens.
We went back inside,
and she climbed up on the couch
to look out the window.
"The moon blew away," she repeated.
But just then the clouds shifted,
and some moonlight shyly peeked down at her.
A giant smile spread over her wonderful little face,
and she pointed out the window,
screaming,
"Moon!"
I smiled back at her, nodding my head yes.
"Moon," I said.
And watching her watch the night sky,
I realized
that eventually all beautiful things will blow away,
and all you can do
is look out your window
and hope the wind blows them
back to you someday.

CHAPTER 23

A MUSEUM OF MEMORIES

My wife and I drove past the house I grew up in
Just as the current owners were pulling in the driveway.
So we introduced ourselves to the man, woman, and two boys,
And they asked us if we would like to look inside
    (Excuse the mess; they were remodeling, etc.)
So my wife and I walked into my childhood,
A museum of memories.
This happened here, I said. That happened there.
I gave them the Cliffs Notes of my life,
Eleven years summed up in a short paragraph.

As we were walking out, finishing the tour,
I suddenly saw my seven-year-old self
sitting on the living room couch
Looking at a picture book about Mexican jumping beans.
I waited for this little boy (who was me) to do something,
To be a memory I remembered,
To be a part of the family stories that get told so often.
You remember how the story goes more than the actual event…

But the boy just sat there,
Lost in the colorful splashes of brown and green.
Then he looked up and noticed my wife and me
And grinned, revealing the tooth I chipped when I was five.

It wasn't really a vision or anything, I know that,
Just my brain playing projector,
But I couldn't help but think that perhaps thirty years ago,
I sat on a couch similar to that one,
In that very room,
Looking at a picture book,

And I wonder if by chance I lifted my head and smiled
For no reason I could think of.

IV. AND I LEAVE YOU WITH THIS

CHAPTER 24

REAL CONVERSATIONS WITH MY KIDS

Me (quizzing Roz for an upcoming test): What are the four forces of nature?
Roz: Water, wind, magnetism, and cardboard.
Me: Uh, no. The fourth one is gravity.
Roz: Oh. Well, the teacher used cardboard to demonstrate gravity.
Me: That doesn't mean cardboard is a force of nature.
Roz: I think it does.

Riley: There's not really a Santa Claus, is there?
Me: No, but there used to be a real person named St. Nicholas.
Riley: What happened to him?
Me: The Tooth Fairy killed him.

Roz: OK, so I'm an evil queen. You throw that, and if it lands inside this circle, then the dragon I'm keeping prisoner can go free. If it lands outside the circle, then I turn invisible, and you have to run and touch every tree in the yard in order to see me again.
Me: Roz, I love your imagination, but this isn't what I meant by "Let's go throw the football back and forth."

Me: Roz, just remember. If you can't be the absolute best at something…
Roz: You can be the absolute worst.
Me: That's not where I was going with that.

Me: Roz, are you crazy?
Roz: Lobster. (Pause) Do you get why I said that? Isn't that hilarious?

Me: What are you doing?
Riley: Studying for a test. It's about light.
Me: Well, don't misbehave, or I'll call the rainbow police, and they'll put you in prism!
Riley: You just ruined science.

Me: Roz, you want some cereal for breakfast?

Roz: Yes.

Me: Yes, what?

Roz: Yes, I do.

Me: Roz, let's do word association. I give you a word, and you tell me the first word that comes to your mind.

Roz: OK.

Me: Dog.

Roz: Dog.

Me: No, it has to be a completely different word. Let's try again. Dog.

Roz: Tomato.

Riley: What was it like in the '80s?

Me: It was a simpler time when we couldn't get enough zippers and a Huey Lewis song could be considered controversial.

Riley: I never know what you're talking about.

Me: Roz, did you have a fun time at Invention Camp?

Roz: Yeah, I hung out with a boy named Aaron.

Me: Oh, yeah? Is he your best friend now?

Roz: We formed an alliance.

Me: What kind of inventions are you guys making?

Riley: At some point, I hope Dora realizes there won't always be three-year-olds around to answer all of her questions for her.

Me (to Riley): What did you just say? Your grammar is not good.

Roz: Hey! Don't you dare talk about my mom's mom like that!

Me: I said "grammar" not "grandma."

Riley: Still, she has a point.

Me: Roz, stop stealing all of Riley's change.

Roz: I'm not stealing it.

Me: Then what do you call it?

Roz: Borrowing it forever.

Riley (at a festival): I hate being nine. I can't decide if I want a tattoo or a balloon animal.

Me: Do you have any last wishes before I throw you out the window?
Roz: Yes, I wish you would not throw me out the window.
Me: Damn.

Roz: I'm a doctor. Now what's wrong?
Me: My elbow really hurts. What can I do to make it better?
Roz: You can do nothing because you're not a doctor. Now shut up and let me fix it.

Riley: What's a vegetarian?
Me: Someone who eats only vegetables.
Riley: That's not me.
Me: No, you're definitely a carnivore. You make vegetarians cry.
Riley: Yeah, because I'd eat them.

Me: Roz, why are you talking so much?
Roz: 'Cause I'm not dead.

Riley: Hey, Dad, why don't boys have babies? I mean, it's not like they don't have butts too.

Riley: I never want to have kids.
Me: Why not?
Riley: Because if one falls over a cliff, I don't want to have to go after it.

Riley: My assignment was to draw something living and something nonliving.
Me: What did you draw that was living?
Riley: A dog.
Me: What did you draw that was nonliving?
Riley: A dead person.

Riley (after my wife playfully smacked her behind): What are you trying to do, give my butt a heart attack?

Roz: Tomorrow at school, I have to write an opinion.
Me: Why don't you write, "My dad is the best"?
Roz: No, it has to be an opinion I agree with.

AND ON THAT NOTE...WE END

Since word got out that I was writing a book called *Daddies Shouldn't Breakdance*, my Facebook wall has been flooded with videos of actual daddies breakdancing. It's as though my friends are saying, "Oh yeah? Here's a dad breakdancing. Now what you got?"

The truth is I will never stop breakdancing (even though I should). I think the biggest mistake we make as parents is forgetting our own childhoods—forgetting what made us weird and sad and scared. What made us belly laugh. What made us slam doors regardless of the consequences.

I tell my kids they have one job in life. Just one. Make the world a better place because they're in it. So far, they seem to be doing really good work. As for me, I'll keep living by that wise old adage: Breakdance like no one's watching.

At least, my kids *hope* no one's watching.

Sincerely,
Phantom J

SPECIAL THANKS

This book would not be possible without the support of so many people. You all have left me without words (a most dangerous position for a writer). I can't thank you enough. In no particular order:

Talcott Starr	Charles Peoples and Randi Arnett	John Walker
Jim and Miriam Kuzma	Pam and David Whitehouse	Joseph M. Knapik
Steve and Connie Sherowski	Sally Williams	Lia Eastep
Eric Dodds	Katie Murphy Russell	Zach Tarantelli
Alexander Sherman Loeb	Monica Klein	Gretchen Hubbe Eyler
Scotty Candler	Jeffrey Tate	Ernest R. Tyler
Rebecca Parsons	Erin and Dylan Ulis	Daniel Osborn
Nicholas and Janet Fletcher	James and Valli Tew	Susan Castro
Gene Dahnke	Jerri Ann Brown	John DeSando
Nickey Winkelman	Christy Grassel	Megan and Mark Markakis
Ann Napoletan	Rick and Candy Hoge	Ann Bostic
John Stegall	Drema Sergent	Shaun and Jennifer Brown
Meg Kirwin	Max Treboni	Jason Dutton
Mark Dahnke	Douglas Baz	Jeffrey Wolf
Michael Pizzuto	Robyn and Doug LaDitka	Brian Rau
Amber Fulmer	Josie Granger	Neal and Leslie Weil
Carlos A. Cook	Dennis and Barb Thompson	Julie Klein
Carrie Russell	Jen Stang Walker	Cathy Lightle Tangey
Charles Seaman	Bill Arrundale	Margaret and Don
Rory Blunt	Cheryl Harrison	Schubbe
Christina D	Pat and Cindy Frey	Edelyn Parker
Gret Otte	Travis Hoewischer	Andy Luttrell
Michelle	Tommy Feisel	Kristin Genchi
Mike Sweet	Erik Tait	Vivian Von Brokenhyman
Rene Dodds Bleidung	Denise Parrish McLellan	Wayne and Christina Lupher
Kaycee Moore	Nina Claussen-Clowes	Karla Manzanilla Ross
Stephen Tew	Dave and Jan Confer	Matt McTeague
Joseph Lorenzo	Trent Reed	Ann Miller Tobin
Matthew Bowshier	Peggy and Steve Yoder	Keith Gibson
Carrie Lynn McDonald	Alan Sacolick	Heather Fidler
Linda Jacobs Widen	Edward Eybel	Bob Makofsky
Canada K	Cathy and Brad Morgan	Larry and Heather Baugess
Max Ink	Rick and Yvonne Brown	Dave Whinham
Sumukh Torgalkar	Phyllis and John Hizey	
Andrew Hartley	Heather Tooill	

41844223R00058

Made in the USA
Middletown, DE
14 April 2019